RUN YOUR
BUSINESS
BETTER

Essential information every business owner should know and use

STEPHEN BARNES

© Stephen Barnes 2017

First published in 2017 by Major Street Publishing Pty Ltd
Contact: E info@majorstreet.com.au | W majorstreet.com.au | M +61 421 707 983

The moral rights of the author have been asserted.

National Library of Australia Cataloguing-in-Publication entry
Creator: Barnes, Stephen, author.
Title: Run your business better: essential information every business owner should
know and use /Stephen Barnes.
ISBN: 9780994545282 (paperback)
Subjects: Small business – Growth.
Small business – Management.
Success in business.
Entrepreneurship.

Internal design by Production Works
Cover design by Simone Geary
10 9 8 7 6 5 4 3 2 1

DISCLAIMER: The information provided in this book is designed to provide
helpful information on the subjects discussed. It is meant to serve as a
comprehensive collection of time-tested and proven strategies.

The information in this book is general in nature and has no knowledge or regard
for the reader's individual circumstances. Summaries, strategies, tips and tricks are
only recommendations by the author, and reading this book does not guarantee
that one's results will exactly mirror our own results. The author has made all
reasonable efforts to provide current and accurate information for the readers of
this book. The author and the publisher will not be held liable for any unintentional
errors or omissions that may be found, or liable for any damages or negative
consequences from any action or application, to any person reading or following
information in this book.

Contents

PART 5: Minimising your risk

PART 6: Essential business resources

Preface

Getting wisdom is the wisest thing you can do!
And whatever else you do, develop good judgment.

(Proverbs 4.7)

Over a number of years, I have worked with an array of businesses and organisations – from publicly listed multinationals to small, not-for-profit organisations. I have worked in industries as diverse as financial markets, horse-breeding, IT software development, hospitality, property development and construction and energy. But all these businesses, though quite different, inherently have exactly the same issues and features.

This book is for all people in business, although it is particularly targeted at those businesses starting out and/or businesses that are floundering. The book does not assume that you have a business education, rather it draws on the one percenters from the world's best business courses, authors and authorities and presents them in a straightforward, easy-to-understand way.

Most of these business owners fall into one of two camps: they are either super enthusiastic but lack structure and certain skills; or have lost their way and are feeling completely overwhelmed.

Throughout these pages, I will take you on a journey, through planning, finance, marketing and managing your risk with the aim of teaching you how to run your business better. Some of the things you read, you may know already – so treat them as a refresher. Others you will wish you had learned earlier.

> *Learn from the mistakes of others – don't make them yourself.*

Some of the things I cover in this book are easy to follow concepts that could have an enormous impact on your business. And, best of all, you don't need to be an accountant, marketing expert or an IT guru to utilise them.

My objective in writing this book is to give you ways to grow your business and regain a life outside your business.

It is not, however, a cure-all of all business problems – it is a coaching tool. Just as a coach isn't on the field and cannot kick the winning goal at a game of footy, I'm not 'on the field' in your business. But I can assist in coaching you to perform at the level you need to achieve your best. This book will give you the tools and strategies, and will hopefully inspire and motivate you, to perform at your best (and bring the best out of you).

Some of what I say in this book may seem a little direct and may be confronting for some readers. When clients come to Byronvale Advisors, they are typically in need of a recovery or a rebuild of their business. Time is of the essence and action is required. Usually they have spent many months, or even years, in denial. The message needs to get through and I need to get them fired up to take action. This is why I take a direct approach. If the content in this book creates a reaction within you, and starts you thinking about your business, you will be in a better place for success (even if you discard the advice)!

I have written this book so that you can read it from cover to cover (which is what I recommend), or you can read the chapter that is of most interest to you in isolation first.

I cover quite a lot of ground, providing an overview of the topics, rather than going into great depth. My aim is to give you enough information to help you to run your business better, to improve the foundation to your business so that you can develop it further.

I genuinely hope this book and the concepts within help you with your business, and I would be pleased to hear your feedback – good, bad and indifferent – just email me at: feedback@byronvaleadvisors.com.

I wish you and your business well.

Stephen Barnes
www.byronvaleadvisors.com
Melbourne, 2017

PART 1

In the beginning

CHAPTER 1

Reasons to be in business

I'm not going to beat about the bush – there are only ever three reasons to be in business and they are:

1. To make money;

2. To have fun; or

3. To make money AND have fun.

If you are not doing one of these three things then shut this book, go and tell your partner that you are not making money and/or having fun, and start looking for paid employment doing something you enjoy.

Or... don't despair, carry on reading and we'll have a look at how to run a business and have fun doing it.

First, let's take a closer look at the three reasons.

REASON 1 – TO MAKE MONEY

Some people regard this first reason as 'capitalistic'. To those people, let me ask you this: 'Does it make sense not to make money?'

You work really hard at producing a product or service and delivering it to the market place. You spend hours of your time doing so – time you could spend having fun or with your family and friends. Why? To earn money so you can use it to provide for your family, secure your future and spend it on things that you enjoy or give you pleasure.

If you are not making money (and not having fun) then try this.

Walk down the road and go to the ATM. Withdraw as much money as you can in $20 notes and put it in a pocket. Continue walking down the street and when you see a homeless person, a charity collector, or just someone who looks like they are having a bad day, give them a $20 note. Continue to do this until you have no money left.

Why would you do this? Because not making money in business is exactly the same as giving money away. The exercise above is actually more effective, you get rid of your money sooner, you feel better having helped people (at least for a short while) than having struggled in your business, and the money is going to people you want to give the money to – not anonymous customers or suppliers that are making money from you.

Your business is not a charity – even if you consider it a charity. Charities may be not-for-profit, but they are also 'not for loss' enterprises.

REASON 2 – TO HAVE FUN!

How much time do you spend on your business? Exclude time you spend sleeping and I'll bet you spend more time on your business than you spend with your family and friends and having fun.

If you are doing this, not making money (though not losing money!), and you enjoy what you are doing, then this is perfectly OK. It is OK as long as you understand that this is why you are in business and as long as it satisfies your other needs and doesn't negatively impact on other parts of your life.

My wish for my children is that they are happy and nice people – it's pretty simple really. After all, not everyone can be a doctor, engineer, lawyer or accountant. How much they earn, how big and flash their houses are and what type of car they drive is not that important. But rather, understanding why they are doing something and being comfortable with that will more likely lead to contentment and happiness.

Doing something that you like is a very valid reason to be in business – it is fun and makes you happy. Lucky you!

REASON 3 – TO MAKE MONEY AND HAVE FUN

Most people will aspire in business to be working for reason 3. They want to enjoy what they do but they'd like to make money too.

Life is a balance and the most successful people achieve a balance between their 'at work' and 'outside work' lives.

I heard this parable of the fisherman and the businessman some time ago and it has stuck with me. Let me share it with you now and you'll understand what I mean.

A large ASX company CEO went on a holiday around Australia – his first holiday for many years. He stopped at San Remo for lunch and a walk along the pier, just as a fisherman was returning with his catch. The CEO complimented the fisherman on his catch and asked him how long he was out fishing. 'Only an hour or so,' said the fisherman.

'Why didn't you stay out longer and catch more fish?' asked the CEO.

'I've caught enough,' said the fisherman.

'What do you do for the rest of the day?' the CEO asked.

'I have a game of chess with my friends at the cafe, then collect my grandchildren from school and take them to sports practice. I then take them home where my wife helps them with their homework as we prepare their dinner. Their parents come for dinner after they finish work, and we have a chat over a cup of tea before they head home. My wife and I then usually go for a walk along the beach and we watch a little TV before retiring to bed.'

The CEO was astonished. 'If you fished longer every day you would make more money, you could buy a bigger boat, or perhaps a fleet. With the size of the catch you would become a price-maker instead of a price-taker and make even more money,' the CEO protested.

'Then what?' asked the fisherman.

'In 10 or 15 years, you'd have made millions and be able to sell the fleet and retire,' the CEO replied.

'Then what?' asked the fisherman.

'You'd be able to have a game of chess with your friends at the cafe, then collect your grandchildren from school and take them to sports practice. Then take them home where your wife would help them with their homework as you prepare their dinner. Their parents would come for dinner after they finished work, and you could all have a chat over a cup of tea before they headed home. Your wife and you would then go for a walk along the beach and watch a little TV before retiring to bed,' he replied.

The CEO farewelled the fisherman and went and had his lunch. While at lunch, he rang the chairman of the board and handed in his resignation.

The point of this parable is that business is not just about maximising the bottom line profit. While profit is important, making profit is a means to an end. Money is important but it is just a tool. Money's value is what you (and only you) intend to do with it.

The fisherman made enough money and enjoyed his life, why would he strive for more?

KEY POINT: Keep front and centre the reason why you are in business. Everything else in the business starts from there.

CHAPTER 2

Let's get the excuses out of the way

There are dozens of reasons or causes espoused as to why a business is struggling, or not meeting original expectations. Let's take a look at some of the common ones upfront:

- *Cash flow* – Often seen as a legitimate reason because statistics like 'seven out of ten businesses fail in the first year because of cash flow' are bandied around.

- *The environment* – 'The retail market is in the doldrums', 'Mining is in the production phase and no longer in the development phase', there's no perfect environment in which to conduct business so stop complaining.

- *Global recession* – This is a tricky one, but how many global recessions come along in a business' lifetime? And, really, I've never seen a global recession that wipes out 100% of businesses in all sectors. Many businesses manage to struggle through a recession – global or local.

- *The appreciation of the currency* – Another good one, often closely followed by the depreciation of currency.

- *My main customer's business failed* – So if you have a smart strategy in place, you will have other customers who will fill the gap – maybe not immediately but in time.

- *Lack of sales* – Well, yes, this will cause business failure, so look at your product, prices, sales team and marketing. The reason is not lack of sales, is it? It's one or all of your product, prices, sales team and marketing.

- *The cost of product went up* – So, that's it? Straight into liquidation? Couldn't you put up your prices, seek a new supplier?

- *Banks have pulled their lending* – Again, this is not really the reason. The reason is that you borrowed too much money and couldn't afford to pay it back.

The reasons your business is not running so well and could run better, which I regard as excuses, can be put into two broad groups – environmental and business. I don't believe any of them are the cause or reason of business failure, instead they are symptoms.

THE SYMPTOMS OF A STRUGGLING BUSINESS

When you wake up in the morning and it is raining, or the sky is blue, what can you do to change that situation? The answer is obviously nothing at all. You have absolutely no control over whether it is going to rain or the colour of the sky. The weather is what it is and you have to just learn to live with that situation.

Likewise, environmental reasons occur in business. If there is a global recession, or the currency is appreciating, or there is a flood or a drought – there is very little you can do about it and you need to learn to live within that environment. Ships don't sink because of water around them. Ships sink because of water that gets in them. Don't let what's happening around you get inside you and weigh you down.

Reasons for your business not running so well can be equally as alarming. It's surprising that anybody would start a business when they hear all the doom and gloom stories about businesses going bust because of lack of cash flow, or the landlord hiked the rent, or their main customer went belly up, or their supplier put up their prices. Again, these are business symptoms – they are not reasons for failure.

THREE VALID REASONS WHY BUSINESSES STRUGGLE

There are, in my opinion, three valid reasons for an ailing business. Your business is not running so well, or could run better, due to one or more of the following:

1. A lack of business skills in the business
2. A lack of attention to applying business skills within the business
3. Spending the majority of the time working *in* the business rather than *on* the business.

Surely not! I hear your cries and jeers. Don't misunderstand what I am saying though. And don't just take it from me. Michael E. Gerber, esteemed author of the bestselling book *E-Myth Revisited,* nailed it when he said:

> 'The assumption is that they understand the business because they understand – and maybe are experts at – the technical work of the business. They think they know the work, they are qualified to run the business.'

What he means is you may be a technical expert or genius practitioner but you also need to know how to run a business. The good news is that running a business is a skill – and skills can be learned. All you need is some devotion and time – this book will help too.

> 'Get comfortable with being uncomfortable. When you start your own company you have to get used to learning how to do things that you don't know how to do.'
>
> – *Heidi Zak, Founder of Thirdlove*

KEY POINT: Business owners must be able to differentiate between the symptoms and the causes of why their business may not be running so well. Then they can get to the bottom of it and start to put things right.

CHAPTER 3

Take the step from practitioner to business owner

Plumbers, electricians and builders go to trade school and undertake both practical and theoretical lessons as part of their training. Software developers, chefs, lawyers, hairdressers and doctors – they all learn the skills to do their job both capably and competently.

They then finish their education or apprenticeship and get their first job and discover they know less than they thought. So they continue learning. After a few years, they're an expert. However, throughout this period they are only learning to become an effective practitioner and not a successful business owner.

Running a business is a separate job and a skill too, and therefore it requires time and investment to learn and develop these skills to become capable and competent to do that job well.

Unfortunately, business skills are not part of a plumbing, hair-dressing or electrical apprenticeship, or part of the curriculum for lawyers, doctors or accountants (yes, that's not a typo, contrary to popular belief, accounting courses do not equip you with the skills to run a business).

A DESIRE TO WORK FOR YOURSELF

If you look at most business start-ups, they either evolve from what was once the business owner's hobby or they are a result of someone wanting to work for themselves.

Think of all the tradies, web-designers, bookkeepers, etc. These people are experts in their fields and have skills, and this is what happens when they go out on their own ill-prepared. They work hard and build up a customer and client base, they get even busier, and then you hear that they've either gone out of business and/or their family life or relationships have broken down.

Were these people incompetent or unskilled at what they do? No. Their mistake was that they did not work *on* their business.

It's human nature to spend more time doing what you enjoy and what you do best. So, our self-employed small business owners gravitate to what they like doing, rather than master the business skills that they lack. The result is that they spend way too much energy *in* their business and not *on* their business.

IT'S REFLECTED IN YOUR PAY

To give you a better understanding of this common problem in business, I'm going to ask you to do an exercise.

Jot down what you would pay a worker, a manager, a director and an owner of your business.

Broadly, the worker is the person doing the job or function. They are the practitioner. It could be a plumber out at a client's premises on a job.

What would you pay a worker? $ _____

The manager is the person co-ordinating the workers and dealing with client complaints and maybe quoting for work.

How much would you pay a manager? $ _____

The director works on strategy and governance.

How much would you pay a director? $ _____

The owner is the person looking after their investment.

How much would you expect an owner to earn? $ _____

You can fill in an hourly rate or an annual salary and they can be just ball-park figures. It's only an exercise, remember.

Now, over the next week, diarise what work you do in 10-minute blocks. Categorise the tasks as worker tasks, manager tasks, director tasks and owner tasks.

At the end of the week analyse the results.

Most businesses that are struggling are doing so because the owner is spending the majority of their time on the worker and manager roles. This is because the jobs that are attributed to these roles are, after all, where the owner has the skills and where they like to gravitate towards, as is only human nature.

However, they are not focusing on the roles and areas of the business that are going to ensure the future of the business and protect their investment.

You may wonder why I asked you to jot down what you would pay people in the roles above. Well, if the majority of your time is spent completing tasks that a worker could be doing, that's what you should be charging out your time at. And this won't be enough to cover your overheads and build your business.

Are you paying yourself too much? How much should you be paying yourself?

WHAT CAN YOU DO?

If you don't have business skills then you will be unable to successfully be in a director role that brings in the big bucks. So you either need to acquire those skills by training yourself – actually learning how to run a business – or you need to employ someone with those skills within your business and pay them the big bucks.

Remember in Chapter 1 when we addressed the three reasons to be in business? Well, you're right, one reason was because it is fun. So, here I'm asking you to distinguish between a hobby and a business. A hobby is something you like doing (it's fun) but its purpose is not to make money. When you decide that you want to take your hobby and make it a business then there needs to be a mental shift. You are no longer a hobbyist or a technician or a practitioner – you are a business owner. As such, your time needs to be weighted towards working on your business.

KEY POINT: You're running a business now, not just working. Businesses fail because the owner doesn't know how to stop being a worker and start being a director. You need to skill up and learn how to run a successful business.

CHAPTER 4

How to manage work life and family life

One of the nice things about working for yourself is the flexibility it gives you with regard to the hours you work. This reason alone is why lots of people head off and start their own business – myself included. 'I'll be able to take the kids to basketball practice', or 'I can have the whole summer holidays off and we'll head off camping'. Sound familiar?

As the business grows, you start working harder – before the family wakes and after they have gone to bed. You take work calls while you're driving in the car on the way to basketball practice. Your family are supportive as they hope you are living your dream.

Father's Day breakfast comes along and you go to school with your children (you can do this because you run your own business, right?). After the breakfast, you are invited to see the kids' work in their classroom. Your eldest daughter has written a poem about Dad and one verse goes: 'Daddy – talk, talk, talk on the phone all day'.

Ah well. Criticism noted!

Next you go off to your youngest daughter's class and she has to answer a quiz on Dad. One question is: 'What does Dad do for a job?'

Your youngest daughter writes down, 'Talks on the phone'.

You've got the message. And wasn't this the complete opposite of what you sought by starting your own business?

You have been isolating yourself from your family and not engaging with your family.

Before you know it, you're not running a business, the business is running you.

EVERY BUSINESS IS A FAMILY BUSINESS

Business can destroy your family life and your family. If you have your own business and you have a family then it's their business too. You might be happy to work 24/7, but they won't be.

Every business is a family business – but it is only a business and not only your entire life.

A business can have a profoundly negative impact on your life if you let it.

It can also serve you and your family well as long as you start working on your business and work more on the strategy and less on the tactical aspects of the business.

While I was reading the Sunday newspaper, I saw an article where Carrie Bickmore from *The Project* was being interviewed by her co-host Waleed Aly. There was a section where Carrie was talking about the juggle of being the best at her job at work and also the best at her 'job' at home. Waleed commented that his wife, Susan Carland, says to him that when he says 'yes' to someone he is saying 'no' to his family, and he pondered why it is easier to say 'no' to his family.

Why is it easier to say 'no' to your family than to a client, customer or someone else?

TIME KEEPS ON TICKING, TICKING, TICKING

A Dad comes home from work and his daughter is about to go to bed. She gives him a cuddle and asks, 'Dad, how much do you earn an hour?'

Stunned, her Dad asks why she needs to know that.

'I just do,' she replied.

'Around $100' her Dad said.

She then asked if she could have $50.

Her Dad, tired, had a short fuse and said, 'Just go to bed – there are enough toys to last a lifetime on the floor!'

The daughter raced off to bed.

After a few minutes, when the Dad had cooled down, he went back to his daughter to tuck her in bed.

'Sorry – I'm tired and have had a hard day. Here is the $50 you asked for,' he said.

'Thanks Dad' she replied and reached under her pillow and pulled out a pile of crumpled notes.

'Why did you need $50 if you already had all this money?' the Dad asked.

'Because I didn't have enough Dad. I've now got exactly $100. Can I buy one hour of your time? Come home early tomorrow please, you haven't had dinner with us for so long,' she asked.

There is only a finite amount of time in a day, in a life, and you are using up that time – second by second.

Time is life; when time ends, life ends.

Time is the most valuable asset you have. You can use that time any way you want, but are you using it rewardingly, intelligently and as intentionally as possible? If not, you're squandering it and failing to appreciate it and living your life oblivious to time passing you by.

> *You can use that time any way you want, but are you using it rewardingly, intelligently and as intentionally as possible? If not, you're squandering it and failing to appreciate it and living your life oblivious to time passing you by.*

VALUE YOUR TIME

It's your failure to manage your time that leads to your business spilling over into family time.

So, what is the value of your time? Are you using time effectively and efficiently? What is the opportunity cost of your time? Failure to recognise and value your time can actually lead not only to the business failing, but you can also lose the other things where your time is valuable – time with your family, friends or doing the things you enjoy.

Years ago, I hired a cleaner at home (actually, two cleaners). It wasn't because I didn't know how to clean, or that I was not capable of cleaning my house. In fact, a bunch of my friends and I were the cleaners of our high school and at university. I hired a cleaner because I worked long hours during the week and often that extended into the weekend. I was single and living by myself, so on the weekend I had to do the cooking, cleaning, gardening, grocery shopping, ironing, etc. So I decided to outsource one of those chores and chose the one I least liked. Cleaning was it.

The opportunity cost of a couple of hours of my time was greater than the actual cost of the cleaner. Have a think about your business – what is the opportunity cost of the time you spend doing a particular task? Can that time be better utilised?

I like playing with websites. I can and have built websites from scratch. But it isn't something that I can do very quickly and I don't necessarily build them as efficiently, or make them as effective, as a website designer could if I were to give them the task.

A paradox I see all the time in small business, in particular, is that the owners do not spend money. I often hear, 'We're a start-up, we don't have the money to spend on a website designer, a bookkeeper, a marketing expert, an IT person, etc.'

But they expect people to spend money at their business – the website designer might need a plumber, the bookkeeper might need a marketing expert, etc.

Do yourself a favour. Work out how best to use your time, what that opportunity cost is and then get people to do the tasks which cost less than your opportunity cost.

And get some family time back.

KEY POINT: If you have a family and you work for yourself then you have a family business. So, you must be fair on your family and make time for them away from your business. One way you can do this is to value your time. Work more *on* the business and pay others to complete tasks that they can do quicker and more efficiently than you can.

PART 2

You have to have a plan

CHAPTER 5

The power of planning

Although this is a generalisation, almost all small businesses – and the majority of medium-sized businesses – don't have a strategic plan, or any plan for that matter.

Some have a financial plan 'because the bank needed one'. But this has long since been filed in the drawer and never been reviewed.

> 'A goal without a plan is just a wish'
>
> *– Antoine de Saint-Exupéry*

So, if most small and medium-sized businesses don't have plans, why should you have a plan for your business?

Let me ask this question: 'Why do most large business have plans?'

Large businesses have plans, not just to keep bankers and investors happy, but they have them as tools to manage their businesses better. They regard plans as a very powerful business tool.

That's why all businesses should have plans – to assist them to manage their business better.

Even the Australian Government's website www.business.gov.au outlines planning as the first step in starting a new business. When you register for an Australian Business Number (ABN), the Australian Taxation Office (ATO) may call you and ask if you have a plan. They may even ask for a business plan if you have losses over consecutive years.

As Benjamin Franklin said, 'If you fail to plan, you are planning to fail.'

WHAT ARE THE ADVANTAGES OF HAVING A BUSINESS PLAN?

Plans help you stay organised and help you co-ordinate your efforts.

Developing plans is not easy. For most small-business owners, their preference is to look at the detail and not the big picture – they are a practitioner and not a leader in the business, remember?

I think the main reason that they don't develop and follow a plan is because they are afraid of failure. 'What would happen if I have a big, hairy, audacious goal and didn't reach it? What would people think?'

A goal or plan will set in place where your business is heading.

When I'm working with business owners, I first assure them that the goals of their business are *their* goals, and no one else cares if they achieve their goals or not. I've never had a client ask me what my goals are and I don't expect I ever will – they just don't care about my goals.

Second, I tell them that not setting a goal or plan is like turning up at the airport without a ticket and not knowing their destination. I ask them, 'What will you do?' and 'How will you do it?' and 'With whom' and 'What do you want out of the trip?'

Third, I assure them that they are more likely to get close to their goal if they first set one. Remember when you were saving up for a car or a house deposit? I bet you had regular savings goals and stuck to a budget. By knowing how much you needed to put away each week or each month, you were more likely to achieve your goal than if you had no goal or plan at all.

PLANS ARE NOTORIOUSLY INACCURATE

A plan is out of date almost as soon as it is completed because things happen along the way that you can't plan for. They can be good things, such as a new client coming on board or implementing a more efficient system that saves you time and money. Or they can be bad (remember the list of excuses in Chapter 2?)

Most plans don't build in slack to account for these unknowns. But the inaccuracy in plans does not make them worthless – in fact it is the process of planning that is most useful.

Planning helps you understand the risks, dependencies and resourcing of your business. As Dwight D. Eisenhower said: 'No battle was ever won according to a plan, but no battle was won without one... plans are useless, but planning is indispensable.'

PLANNING WITH STRATEGY IN MIND

I hope by now I've allayed your fears of planning and you're keen to develop a plan for your business. You should be convinced of the importance of a plan by what I have described so far in this chapter. Now I'll go through why you need a particular type of plan – a strategic plan.

A strategic plan is the foundation or primary plan for your business. It is your roadmap for the medium term – approximately the next three to five years – and establishes where the business is headed. It sets out the organisational vision, mission and values and focuses the energy, time and resources of the business in the same direction.

It points to specific results that are to be achieved and establishes a course of action for achieving them. A strategic plan also helps the various work units within a business align themselves with common goals.

Without a strategic plan, a business will wander aimlessly and priorities will change constantly as employees, and business owners, become confused about the purpose of their jobs.

Businesses that perform at the highest levels have a formalised strategic plan in place and implement it well. Once you have developed your strategic plan, the key to making it work is to commit to seeing it through and implementing it across all areas of the business.

THE STRATEGIC PLANNING PROCESS

Building a strategic plan is not difficult and it should be a rewarding experience. Think of the strategic planning process as being like planning an overseas family holiday. First, you'll need to know where you want to go and why. Then you can create the details of your trip, such as the length of time you will spend away, how much time you will be off work for, how much the airfares will cost and what activities you will do.

With a strategic plan, it's more about defining your:

• mission;

• values; and

• vision.

Get these right and your business won't fail. Let's consider each in turn, and I will show you how to design your strategic plan.

Mission statement

Your mission statement addresses the 'why we exist' question. It determines why you are in business and is a statement of your business' purpose. It focuses directly on the business you are presently in and the customer needs you are presently striving to meet. It determines what is 'in' and what is 'out'.

The mission statement should serve as the foundation for everything you do – both for current day-to-day operations and as a foundation for future decision-making. It should also be concise. As Peter Drucker said, 'Your mission should fit on a t-shirt'.

To give you an idea of what your mission statement should say, here are a few mission statements from well-known organisations:

* *Google.* 'To organize the world's information and make it universally accessible and useful.'

* *Warby Parker.* 'Warby Parker was founded with a rebellious spirit and lofty objective: to offer designer eyewear at a revolutionary price, while leading the way for socially-conscious businesses.'

* *International Red Cross.* 'To provide relief to victims of disaster and help people prevent, prepare for and respond to emergencies.'

It is quite clear in these examples why all of these organisations exist.

You cannot determine where your business is going without first gathering some data about why you exist and where you are now. Completing the following steps will help you create your mission statement.

1. Identify the strategic issues your business faces.

2. Conduct an environmental scan or PEST analysis, which covers the following variables:
   - Political (includes legal and regulatory)
   - Economic
   - Social (demographics)
   - Technological.

3. Gather and review internal feedback – from key stakeholders and internal reporting.

4. Conduct a competitive advantage analysis by asking questions such as 'What do you do best?' 'What do you do or potentially do better than similar organisations?'

5. Define your customer segments.

6. Do a SWOT analysis:
   - Strengths – what does your business do well?
   - Weaknesses – what are the limitations your business faces in developing or implementing a strategy?
   - Opportunities – how can your business act upon potential opportunities and benefit from them?
   - Threats – are there external conditions or barriers that may prevent your business from reaching its objectives?

Values statement

Next, consider your values.

Values clarify what your organisation stands for and believes in and the behaviours you expect to see from your employees and yourself as a result. They are the beliefs that guide the conduct, activities and goals of the business, and they establish what you do and what you stand for.

The values of a business form the cornerstone of its organisational culture and are to be upheld throughout your organisation.

As such, when you are defining your organisation's values, it is important to get input from all the staff involved in the business. An anonymous survey will get the best response from your staff as values are personal, and people need to feel they can share their values without any influence or judgment.

Having input from everyone involved in your business means the values statement has meaning and is not just a list of ideas that no one is interested in. Some questions that you might ask when considering your values are:

- What are the guiding principles for how we treat each other and our customers?

- What are the key non-negotiables that are critical to the success of the business?

- What are the guiding principles that are core to how we operate in this business?

- What behaviours do you expect to see?

The outcome is a values statement that articulates what your business believes in and a statement that holds true. It should comprise five to seven core and shared values.

You may think that values are a given but when they are articulated they can be used as a guide for reinforcement, training, rewards and consequences for poor behaviour and alignment of goals.

It is not sufficient to determine your organisation's values and just post them on the business website – they need to be integrated into the day-to-day operations of the business. This way the values will come to life and become real.

Years ago, ANZ Bank implemented a hugely successful cultural change project called 'Breakout'. Starting at the top of the organisation and then moving down to the rank-and-file, staff went through a program that addressed their values and then the values of the bank. These values underpinned everything the bank did and were a guiding principle to training, staff remuneration and roles. The internal staff satisfaction levels soared as the cultural transformation occurred. At that time, the customer satisfaction also soared. Essentially what ANZ Bank did was address the four value-based questions above and then integrated them into the day-to-day operations of the bank.

Vision statement

Using the mission statement and the values statement, and the data you have gathered, you can now determine where you want to be, i.e. your business' goal and your vision for the business.

Your vision statement answers the question 'Where is the business going?' If it is not clear where the business is going, you cannot create a plan.

Vision statements are aspirational big hairy audacious goals (BHAGs).

Here are some well-known BHAGs from recognisable sources:

- *John F Kennedy.* 'We will put a man on the moon before the end of the decade and bring him back.'

- *Microsoft.* 'A computer on every desk and in every home using great software as an empowering tool.'

- *Amazon.* 'Our vision is to be earth's most customer centric company; to build a place where people can come to find and discover anything they might want to buy online.'

In order to come up with a strong vision statement, consider the following key elements:

- *Future casting.* The vision statement should provide a picture of what the future looks like for the business long term. It tries to envision your company's future.

- *Short and sweet.* The statement should be two sentences maximum. It is an elevator pitch but just between two floors.

- *Clear and visible.* You need to be able to see your business at its 'goal'. The words cannot be open to interpretation.

- *Audacious and ambitious.* The vision statement is a dream beyond what you currently think is possible.

- *Motivating.* It inspires you, your staff and your customers.

- *Purpose driven.* It gives a reason or purpose for doing what you are doing.

- *Inspiring.* The language is engaging.

- *Capitalises on core competencies.* It builds on the business' current competencies.

Not all businesses get their vision statement right. Here are a couple of not-so-great vision statements:

> *'Build the best product, cause no unnecessary harm, use business to inspire and implement solutions to the environmental crisis.'*

> *'Provide maximum value for our shareholders whilst helping our customers to fulfil their dreams.'*

While the first vision is ambitious and even inspirational I still have no idea what 'best product', 'no unnecessary harm' and 'inspire and implement solutions' really mean or what it looks like.

The second example could apply to any company, it's not unique or inspiring. Who would know that this was an insurance company's vision statement?

It is important not to confuse mission and vision.

A mission explains *why* you exist, your purpose.

The vision explains *where* you are heading, your goal.

In the diagram below 'A' is where the business is now. 'B' is your vision or goal.

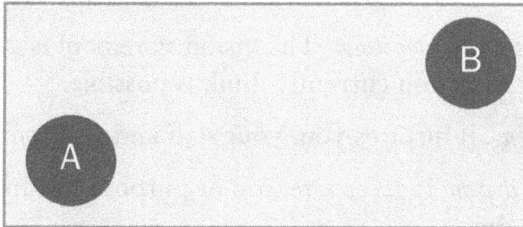

The box is your mission. I call it a paddock, and the type of farm is determined by what is in the paddock. Make sure that the only things your business does is within the paddock, or mission, and therefore also make sure your vision is within the paddock or mission.

When it comes to creating your vision statement, you have a few options. It can be:

- *Quantitative.* It includes words to the effect of, 'to have 10,000 users of our software in ten years' time'.

- *Competitive.* You might be trying to outdo competitors and state something such as, 'to be the only provider of cloud-based accounting software in the SME market in Australia.'

- *Superlative.* Your vision is to be the most exceptional or outstanding such as, 'the number one volume building company in Melbourne.'

To put a vision statement together, get as many of your staff on board as you can. The vision statement is not about delivering the vision to your staff but is about getting them engaged and buying into the vision.

Gather everyone in a room and put them into small groups, then ask the following question, 'Where do you all think the company should be in, say, five years time?' Then, tell everyone that your business is going to be on the cover of the most prestigious magazine for your industry, and you want to know what the headline will be, what are the pictures, what are people saying about your business?

Use this information to come up with the vision statement (just one sentence). The rest of the information can be used as a vision description.

Lastly, know what mountain you are climbing. When you get to the top you want to make sure you have climbed the right mountain.

KEY POINT: Once you get over the fear of planning, you need to tackle strategic planning. The key ingredients of a strategic plan are your business' mission, values and vision statements. These are more than just statements – you need to embed them in your workforce, in all parts of your organisation.

CHAPTER 6

Strategic objectives

Your mission, values and vision have to be supported by strategic objectives. Many businesses miss this step in their strategic planning. We discussed mission, values and vision in the previous chapter, so here I want to talk about objectives as I guide you in completing your strategic plan.

OBJECTIVES

Listing your objectives is the next step in developing your general, high-level methods or strategic objectives that you will use to reach your vision. Compiling this list will determine the most direct or clearest path from where you are now to where you want to be.

Let's revisit the paddock diagram from the previous chapter.

Your objectives should set you on a straight course to get from A (your business now) to B (where you want to be).

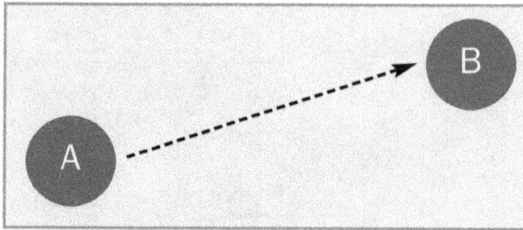

Start by articulating the organisation-wide strategy and then put in place a set of manoeuvres or guard rails to keep you as close to the straight or direct path to reach your business' goal or vision. This answers the 'how' question – how is your business going to reach its vision?

The strategic objectives are high-level, general statements that guide and cover a range or set of activities. They are used to operationalise the mission statement and help to provide guidance on how the business can fulfil or move towards its vision.

The strategic objectives, like the vision, are long-term in nature. They should collectively address all areas of the business – finance, people, customers, marketing, sales, process and operations.

A structure you may want to follow to develop your strategic objectives is:

Action + detail + metric + unit + deadline

Let's take a look at an example. One of your strategic objectives might be to 'expand our international operations into three new markets by December 2020.'

You will notice the above statement is high-level and does not address the subset of tasks and actions needed to deliver the objective or strategy. Try to keep your strategic objectives to a sentence that is easy to remember and understand.

ACTIONS

Your strategic objectives now need to be broken down into actions or tasks that can be converted into specific performance targets. They have to address what needs to be completed in the short term to achieve the strategic objectives.

To formulate actions, you may like to use the SMART principles:

- *Specific.* Answer the questions 'how much?' and 'what kind?' with each action.

- *Measurable.* Without being measurable, your objectives will lack accountability and be just good intentions.

- *Attainable.* While an aspirational goal may inspire you, if the action is not attainable all you are doing is setting up for failure.

- *Responsible person.* Each action needs to have a champion to ensure the action is 'actioned'.

- *Time specific.* Set a realistic time when the action needs to be delivered.

COMPETITIVE ADVANTAGE

All businesses need to know their competitive advantage in order to succeed. In other words, what is your business best at? If you don't have a clear idea of this, why will clients and customers use your products and services?

To establish your business' competitive advantage, you need to consider what the characteristics of your business are that allow it to meet your customers' needs better than your competition? It may take some time to narrow this down. To get started, you should use this simple formula:

Business name + best at + why

For example: Joe's Plumbing + residential plumbing services + on time, courteous service. Once you know what your competitive advantage is, it needs to be built into your strategic plan.

Many businesses that I have worked with or consulted to have been failing because they have been unable to articulate their competitive advantage.

This is a vital step in your planning process and it is one that is often missed.

MEASURING SUCCESS AND REVIEWING YOUR PLAN

The final part of the process is to put in place a system for measuring success. These are often called key performance indicators (KPIs) and they are key to ensuring that the actions that will move your organisation through the strategic plan to the vision are on track – hopefully along that straight line.

It is important to use actual measures. These will ensure accountability. They serve to make sure the actions are aligned, or realigned, to the tasks and strategic objectives. Strategic planning is not a case of 'set and forget'. A review of your strategic plan is often thought of as something you do down the track, when you have implemented the strategic plan.

This is partly true. However, it should also be incorporated into the building phase. Remember that the strategic plan outlines how you are going to move from the present status to where you want to be – or your vision.

It is vital that during that journey there are regular reviews of the strategic plan to ensure the plan is still relevant and that the actions undertaken are not deviating from the mission and the strategic objectives to attain the vision.

Strategic plans are guidelines and not rules.

Ask the following types of questions when you review your strategic plan:

- Will your goals be achieved in the timeframes in the plan? If not, why not?

- Should the timeframes and deadlines be modified? Why should they be modified?

- Are the goals and actions still realistic and relevant? Should they be changed?

- Should there be a change in focus to put more emphasis on achieving the goals, or a particular goal?

The point is to reaffirm the mission and vision, and then ensure you are not diverting from the straight line between the two.

Remember that the strategic plan outlines how you are going to move from the present status to where you want to be – or your vision.

KEY POINT: It's all well and good having a strategic plan, but without a set of objectives to guide you when you're working towards your vision, you are unlikely to get there. The objectives are part of the plan – without them you have a mission, value and vision statement.

CHAPTER 7

Don't leave your plan on a piece of paper

If you've read this far, you've probably started to give some serious thought to your strategic plan, so I need to remind you now of the importance of implementing your plan. Your strategic plan is more than a piece of paper. It is not a tick-the-box exercise – it has to be much more than that.

Executing your strategic plan is as important, if not more important, than developing your strategy. It moves it from a document that sits on a shelf getting dusty to actions that drive organisational change and growth.

Implementation of your plan addresses the who, where, when and how, whereas the strategy addresses the what and why questions.

My experience has shown me that you need to review and track the goals and objectives that you have set for your business, otherwise your plan will be regarded as a once-off exercise rather than something that is ongoing.

The plan is not to be only discussed annually at a 'weekend retreat'. It is to be communicated regularly and widely. Unless everyone is told about it, how can you expect them to understand it and to contribute to it? Lack of ownership of the plan is a big risk. If people do not take responsibility for the plan, it will continue to be business as usual.

Another risk to the successful implementation of your plan is that it is regarded as the 'Oh my God' plan – it's too large, too grand and the goals and actions required to implement it are too numerous, and it's difficult to prioritise which steps to take first. By not considering the plan's implementation it is seen as an end in itself, and how it is going to be implemented is not discussed during the planning process.

AVOID THE PLANNING PITFALLS

One of the challenges with implementing your plan is that it can be hard to track progress. Sure, you can ask for progress reports, but often it's tempting just to measure what's easy and not what is important. When this happens, momentum stalls and everyone gets frustrated.

To get around this, make sure you ask people in your organisation to be accountable. With accountability comes empowerment. If they are going to be made responsible for helping to successfully implement the plan, then you need to give them authority and the tools necessary to impact the relevant measures.

HOLD AN ANNUAL REVIEW

Despite having warned you of only reviewing your plan once a year, it is important that, as well as the regular reviews, you do hold an annual strategic review and provide all stakeholders with an annual update.

Don't invite everyone to this update. Too many people create 'management by committee' which is not conducive to well thought out decision-making and strong leadership. However, you might want to consider having a cross-section of your employees attend.

Other tips for holding a successful annual strategy update are:

- *Address the 'elephant in the room'.* This should be done prior to the annual update. Don't let the 'elephant' disrupt the annual update and become the focus of the session.

- *Do your homework.* Come armed with facts and don't waste time during the update conducting research on the go.

- *Use a facilitator.* This is crucial. A good facilitator will keep the meeting on track and keep the process moving towards the desired outcome. I have never seen a good strategic day without a facilitator.

- *Focus on the agenda and not the outcomes.* While getting through the agenda is what it usually takes to get a completed plan, focusing on outcomes is more important than just ticking a box by completing the agenda. One of the best strategy sessions I've ever attended was set over two and a half days and we got through three of the five agenda items. However, they set up the foundation better, and the session was more fruitful.

- *Explain the process.* The facilitator should explain the process so that everyone is on the same page and no-one is left behind. When this happens, the meeting can focus on outcomes and not get side-tracked or derailed. Again, the reason we got through three of five agenda items was because the facilitator would not move on and leave anyone behind (and no he was not ex-military).

- *Don't assume everyone thinks like you.* Walk in other people's shoes. Not everyone has the same preferences as you. Also, no matter how hard you try, you cannot change people's preferences. Learn to work with those preferences rather than try to change them.

- *Don't overlook life after the meeting.* Going back to business as usual, as if you never had a strategic planning meeting, is a waste of everyone's time and money and makes it virtually impossible to get participation and engagement in the future. Don't let this happen!

KEY POINT: Don't leave your business plan in the desk drawer. It is almost like a living document – you need to review it regularly and it will evolve as you respond to external and internal changes. When you hold your annual strategy update meeting, make sure you give it the best chance of success.

CHAPTER 8

The importance of your operational plans

Strategic planning is not the only type of planning a business owner must undertake. You only have to Google 'business plan templates' to get an idea of the number of varieties of plans you can put together.

Resourcing plans are another key planning tool. They aim to identify current and future resources your business needs. Resource plans are common in the project management sphere but are applicable to every business – after all, isn't your business just a big project? Resources for a resources plan may be human resources (people), but also technology, office or warehouse space, vehicles, etc. With a business, it is important to understand the timing of when resources need to be acquired and the impact their acquisition has on the financial plan, cash flow forecast and the overall strategic plan.

If you are running a business, one of your most powerful plans is your financial plan. A key skill you have to learn if you are running a business is to understand the 'numbers' that drive the business. You cannot just bury your head in the sand and continue doing what you like doing and what you do best.

Let's continue your business education by taking a look at the all-important financial plan – or budget.

Your financial plan takes a snapshot of your business at one point–in-time. It is based on current information (information available at the time of drafting the financial plan) and takes into account future assumptions.

There are two keys to a good financial plan.

First, the assumptions used in the financial plan must be valid and justifiable. If you cannot justify every figure in your plan, the credibility is severely compromised, and you have also probably not put enough robust thought and questioning into the development of the plan. Part of the reason you put plans together is not just to arrive at the end result, but rather the process of questioning and validating while you compile the financial plan gives you a greater understanding of what's going on in the business.

Second, you need to remember that the financial plan is only made at a point in time. You should not be constantly changing the budget throughout the period of the budget. If things change, and they always do, then use another form of report, which larger businesses often use, that is a rolling forecast. Unless you really like number-crunching or have dedicated accounting staff to do this for you, a rolling forecast might be a step too far. Again, a large part of the value of the financial plan is actually the process of putting the plan together.

A large part of the value of the financial plan is actually the process of putting the plan together.

CASH FLOW FORECAST

'Happiness is a positive cash flow'

– Fred Adler

Fred Adler was a pioneer of venture capital markets in the USA and this is his most famous epigram. Fred Adler had various epigrams that some called Adler's Laws. They all held little regard for the 'glitz and glamour' people like to portray with their businesses – boozy lunches, big flash offices, glossy brochures, etc. What was important to Fred were the things that made the business successful, such as:

- being able to generate more cash than was spent; and

- having the cash where and when you need it.

He regarded both as vital to a business' survival.

I find the cash flow forecast the most useful report for the day-to-day management of a business. Unlike most accounting reports that review what has occurred in the past, or the 'sins of the profit' such as the profit and loss statement or balance sheet, the cash flow forecast is a proactive tool.

I had a client who took three months to actually put the effort into compiling a cash flow forecast for their business. They wanted to bury their head in the sand (it would have taken me an hour!) However, once they did have a cash flow forecast, it not only helped them manage their cash flow but it gave them much better insights into the business. It showed them the size of the pipeline of sales and debtor receipts they needed to generate each week to cover the cash outflows and it showed up which creditor payments they needed to try and push out and which debtors they needed to chase.

With their cash flow statement in place, this client had a terrible shock. They realised that they did not have a plan, or the ability, to generate the required cash to cover their outgoings. They needed to make some hard decisions regarding what they were spending cash on, how they were managing their working capital and how they could increase and diversify sales income.

Most accounting software packages can produce a simple cash flow forecast; however, it should be used only as a starting point.

Here are some questions to ask when building a cash flow forecast:

- Are all invoices in the accounting system? (Make sure they are not sitting unopened on someone's desk, or filed in a drawer or a rubbish bin!)

- Are the payment and receipt dates reflective not of the payment terms but of when they are actually expected to be paid and received?

- Are all cash items (GST, wages, taxes, superannuation) included?

Include the GST inclusive amounts in your cash flow forecast and not the GST exclusive amounts that you put in your financial plan or profit and loss statement.

TIP: Only include items in your cash flow forecast that you are certain of.

Don't for instance put projected sales into the cash flow forecast – only put the sales you have actually made. When you only put in the cash items that you are certain of, then you will see the cash flow gap and you can start getting busy working out how you can close the gap.

For some clients, I have overlayed a simple risk reporting tool on the cash flow forecast. It looks at the cash you have today and the cash you forecast to have say in 12 months time and puts a traffic light system in place. This is useful for board reporting as the board can quickly assess the level of focus required on the cash flow:

- green = all good;

- amber = ask management what their strategy is to manage the cash flow; and

- red = stop everything and focus attention on fixing the cash flow.

KEY POINT: Owners bury their heads in the sand when it comes to financial planning. The most useful business tool in financial planning is a cash flow forecast.

PART 3

Knowing your numbers

CHAPTER 9

Knowing what to charge

The price that you set for your products and services is one of the most crucial decisions you have to make in a business, so you'll forgive me for dedicating quite a few pages to this issue in this book.

Pricing requires thought and an understanding of your customers or clients, the market, the environment and your competitors. Entrepreneurs and new businesses often give too little thought to this highly complex matter and the consequences can be dire. Set your prices too low and you are leaving money on the table. Set your prices too high and nobody will buy your product or service. The right price is the maximum the customer or client is willing to pay.

THE PSYCHOLOGY OF PRICING

Before setting a price for a product or service, you need to understand what the price indicates to your target customer or client.

Price can indicate quality or value and, subject to having no other information, we look to price first to shed light on the quality. Therefore, products and services that are more expensive are perceived to be better quality, and products and services priced lower are perceived to be of lower quality.

Businesses use price to communicate something about their product or service. They may lower the price to communicate value for money, or raise the price to communicate quality or prestige. Of course, neither of these may be true, but it is a message that the business is trying to communicate.

Pricing also needs to be consistent with the other brand elements. For example, if you are trying to price for exclusivity then the marketing, packaging, sales pitch, etc., need to also reflect the exclusivity of the brand.

Look at your own behaviour.

Did you buy a coffee today? How much did you pay for it and why? Do you pay more for a coffee to have at the cafe than you do for a takeaway in a disposable cup? Do you pay more at a boutique cafe than at a fast food outlet? Did your coffee also come with a biscotto and a cube of raw sugar? The price charged communicates the perceived quality or value to the target customer.

Let me demonstrate this through examples.

It's not about the coffee

At home, sitting on your bench, you probably have a container of supermarket bought freeze dried coffee. You drink it every day but it really doesn't make that great a coffee and certainly not when you compare it to the freshly ground, tempered and barometrically infused coffee made by a barista.

One day you decide to go to the most expensive restaurant in town for coffee and dessert. You look at the menu and see that to have both coffee and dessert requires you to take out a second mortgage to pay for it (well not quite, but you get where I'm coming from). You decide not to have the dessert and just order the coffee. The coffee arrives and it is the best coffee you've had in a long time. Unbeknown to you, though, this restaurant makes its coffee using the supermarket bought freeze dried coffee. But you thought the coffee was great – why?

First, because the price communicated quality to you – when have you have a bad $10 cup of coffee?

Second, because this restaurant has the best reputation or brand in town and brands change perceptions. Perceptions are peoples' reality. You know this is the best restaurant and the food and beverages are only the best, so you think the coffee is great even though in reality, it really isn't.

The coffee was served to you in a very expensive fine-china cup, in a restaurant with expensive decor, in the expensive part of town and with Andrea Bocelli playing through a sound system costing the same as an average house. The 'packaging' of the coffee also affects your perception of the coffee. People think with their eyes.

The waiter or waitress who served you the coffee was immaculately groomed, extremely polite and knowledgeable, and available and 'present'. The perceived value that came from buying the coffee was not just about the product or the price, it was also the service and the engagement with the customer.

Customer engagement is key

Another example of this comes from my childhood.

My parents were in the market to buy a brand new car. One Saturday, my Dad was out in the garden and my Mum called out saying it was time to leave to look at cars. We all hopped in the car and Dad was still wearing the clothes he had been wearing in the garden.

We arrived at the car dealership and the salesperson kept directing Mum and Dad to the second-hand cars. Mum and Dad didn't want a second-hand car so they left and walked across the road to another car dealership with a different brand of cars. Within an hour, Mum and Dad had signed up to buy a new car.

So, what was the difference between the two products? Not much really – both cars had similar features and were priced much the same, but the difference in the ability to engage with the customer resulted in the second dealership winning the sale.

You can price higher and you will sell more if you engage with your customers and form a relationship with them even if, going back to my coffee example, the product may be inferior.

> *You can price more and you will sell more if you engage with your customers and form a relationship with them.*

So, in summary, on the psychology of pricing:

- *Pricing should be about value – real or perceived.* Get customers or clients to focus on value and what you can do for them and they will stop focusing on cost.

- *Focus on how people feel and not how people think.* Connecting with customers or clients will bypass objections and resistance and let you focus on the relationship. It stops you having to justify your price and what you are worth and allows you to sell to people.

- *How you communicate with customers and clients affects the pricing.* The setting, atmosphere and your ability to pay attention to the details communicates to the customer or clients and sets their expectations.

- *Customers and clients are not rational.* Keep in mind pricing needs to reflect people's behaviours.

PRICING OBJECTIVES

A pricing objective is essentially your pricing goal. It is what you are trying to achieve by the way you price your products or services. There are four common pricing objectives:

1. Profitability building

2. Volume boosting

3. Matching competition

4. Prestige pricing.

Let's look at each of these in turn.

Profitability building

Profitability building is sometimes called survival pricing because your pricing objective is on building profitability, and to do this you start by looking at costs. Costs include both variable and fixed costs. You need to look at both to find out what it actually costs to make a product or provide a service.

Variable costs refer to how much it costs to make a particular product. These are sometimes referred to as material costs, cost of goods sold or direct costs.

Fixed costs are all the other costs associated with operating your business that are not directly associated with producing the actual product or service. These include electricity, rent and other office costs. Fixed costs are also known as overheads or indirect costs.

So, when you have a profitability objective, you are looking to ensure that the pricing will cover all the costs – both variable and fixed. In this situation, you may use a breakeven analysis or marginal cost analysis to determine the price.

The problem with the profitability pricing method is that it doesn't consider the following important factors:

- Will the consumer pay that price for the product or service?

- What are your competitors charging for the same product or service?

- What is the psychology of the consumer?

It is, however, easy to rationalise and compute profitability pricing and so it is often used by start-up businesses and small businesses.

Volume boosting objective

Our second pricing objective is to sell more units and not be overly concerned at profitability per unit. At some point, though, even with a volume-boosting pricing objective, you will need to be overall profitable.

Generally, you make only a small amount of money per unit using this strategy. A common example of businesses that adopt this type of pricing is supermarkets, which sell a high volume of product with very low profit per unit.

To complicate things further, there are several different pricing strategies that can be used to boost volume. They are:

- *Penetration pricing.* This strategy is where you charge extremely low prices (at least initially) to increase market share. By charging a low price, you lower the pricing hurdle for consumers to purchase the product. It is used to create a market niche. Low-cost airlines use penetration pricing. They carve out a particular part of the overall market that other participants are unwilling to compete in. Another example of penetration pricing is when a new product is launched on the market and the aim is to gain a share of the overall market. Once market share is established then prices may be gradually increased.

- *Everyday low pricing.* This approach allows consistent discounting. An example in Australia is Bunnings with its slogan 'We won't be beaten on price'. Bunnings does not vary its prices often and does not have sales on products. They consistently offer the product at the low price. Customers expect that the prices will be the same from one day to the next and do not have to wait until a particular day to get a lower price. For the seller, this also eliminates some of the volatility in sales as the consumer is not waiting for a sale or discount day.

- *High/low pricing.* This involves discounting prices on certain products to increase overall traffic. You discount a product for a short amount of time to encourage a reaction to drive traffic to your business. Department stores use this kind of pricing often. They may run a promotion for one day offering a 25% discount on children's clothing. The next day, the children's clothing is back to full price and then they might run a promotion discounting homewares for a day.

The problem with high/low pricing is that consumers come to expect that products will be discounted and will wait for the discount or sale. What's more, trying to move from high/low pricing to everyday low pricing is very difficult as the high/low pricing becomes ingrained in consumers' behaviours.

- *Loss leader pricing.* With this strategy, businesses price items temporarily below cost – again to increase volume or traffic, or to drive sales in other products. Printers are an example of this. Printers themselves are very cheap to purchase but ink per ounce is more expensive than gold. Printer manufacturers and retailers loss-lead with the printer sale, knowing that to use the printer you'll have to purchase the ink cartridges or toners. And this is where they mark up higher. They make their profits on the ink and don't worry too much what they make on the printers themselves.

Matching competition

Our third pricing objective is simply to price the same as the market leader. This approach is used when you are aiming to position yourself, your company or your product as similar to a company or product that has the greatest market share.

You are piggy-backing off the competitor and trying to create the perception that your company or product has the same quality, prestige or value as that of your competitor.

There are two strategies used with this pricing objective:

- price the same as the competitor to lift the value of your product; or

- price the same as your competitor but offer a better product or service.

This objective is not recommended for small companies going up against large companies. My company, Byronvale Advisors, would not be using this pricing strategy when competing with the multinational management consulting firms. Use matching competition pricing if you are going up against smaller or similar sized companies, you offer a superior product or service and can withstand an economic loss for a short period.

PRICING FOR PRESTIGE

Finally, let's consider the pricing for prestige method. The objective of this approach is to communicate to customers that your products or services are the best quality or that they are scarce. We use a pricing strategy called price-skimming. Price-skimming involves offering products or services at 'premium' prices. Remember that high prices communicate quality.

Price-skimming is a useful strategy when you are first to market or there isn't a substitute product. Companies also use this strategy when trying to recover research and development costs or large initial marketing or regulatory costs. Pharmaceutical companies launching a new drug might engage in price-skimming for instance.

However, there are two caveats. First, the product or service must be worthy of the price, and second the product or service must not be easily copied such that it could be produced and sold at a lower price.

MARGINS AND MARK-UPS

Margin and mark-up are the same thing, right? Well they sound similar and are often both used to describe a method of pricing. But I have news for you. Not only are they two different things but not understanding each one and the differences between them could get you into financial trouble.

So, here's what each one is:

- *Margin.* The sales price less cost of goods sold (it can be expressed as a dollar amount or a percentage).

- *Mark-up.* The amount by which the cost of a product is increased in order to derive the selling price.

If you make a mistake in the application of margin or mark-up, it can lead to you setting a price that is too high or too low – especially when you express it as a percentage.

Let's show you the difference using some common numbers.

If:

Selling price = $100

Costs = $70

The profit on this product is $30.

So what is the margin and what is the mark-up?

- *The margin* is $100 less $70 = $30 or a 30% margin (margin divided by selling price).

- *The mark-up* is the amount from which the cost is increased to get the selling price, so the mark-up = $30 ($70 + $30 = $100), but as a percentage the mark-up is $30/$70 or 42.85%.

Mark-ups are often used in retail businesses where products have a 'targeted' return. By this I mean the business is looking to make a certain amount of money on every sale of a particular product. Again, the level of mark-up is determined by your pricing objectives. A low mark-up may be used if you have a volume pricing objective and a high mark-up may be used if you have a prestige pricing objective.

Mark-ups are often used in retail businesses where products have a 'targeted' return.

If the difference between the two concepts continues to cause trouble for the sales staff, consider printing cards that show the mark-up percentages to use at various price points and distribute the cards to the staff. The cards should also define the difference between the margin and mark-up terms and show examples of how margin and mark-up calculations are derived.

DISCOUNTING

You should proceed with caution when using the discounting method. Some businesses are too quick to rush to discount before understanding or being aware of the impact the discounting will have on cash flow and profitability.

Let's use an example again to explain:

Current sales = $1,500,000

Cost of goods sold = $900,000

Gross profit = $600,000

Gross margin = 40%

Proposed discount = 20%

Therefore, after discounting:

Discounted sales = $1,200,000

Cost of goods sold = $900,000

Gross profit = $300,000

Gross margin = 25%

To maintain the original gross profit of $600,000 worth of sales, you would need to increase sales volume to $2,400,000. If the volume is not achieved, the shortfall directly impacts on your profitability.

(Discounting also affects working capital but we'll save that until later in the book.)

Some businesses are too quick to rush to discount before understanding or being aware of the impact the discounting will have on cash flow and profitability.

WHICH PRICING OBJECTIVE IS BEST FOR YOUR BUSINESS?

The answer to this question is that it depends on your customers, and it may also depend on which segment of your customer base you are selling to.

For example, say you are a plumber with a diverse client base – parents, volume builders, schools, etc. How you price to each of these segments of your market may be different. When you are pricing to parents, you may use the profitability objective with a high mark-up on a time and materials basis. Pricing to the volume builder segment may use the matching competition objective and on a price-per-house basis rather than a time-and-materials basis.

Pricing may also be influenced by the channel through which you sell the product, e.g. via a retail store or online. If, say, you are a florist, you may have a price for a bouquet of flowers that you sell in-store and a different price for the same bouquet of flowers when you sell it online.

Customers also accept different price points for the same product.

Let's use the example of buying a can of soft drink. There are different places and ways to buy a can of soft drink. You will most likely get the lowest price (say 50 cents a can) if you buy a case from the supermarket. You would pay more at the convenience store, at a vending machine, cafe, restaurant and hotel mini bar. The hotel mini bar may charge $5 a can – a 1,000% price differential for the same product.

KEY POINT: Businesses that don't know what to charge will struggle. You must have a clear pricing objective. Consider all four pricing strategies in this chapter to help you make your pricing decisions.

restaurant bar. The hotel might one day charge $5 ... a 1,000% ... are differentiated for the same product.

KEY POINT: Businesses that don't know what to charge will struggle. You must have a clear pricing objective. Consider all four pricing strategies in this chapter to help you make your pricing decisions.

CHAPTER 10

Pricing rules for start-ups and entrepreneurs

Chapter 9 was more comprehensive because I needed to get you to look at pricing from all the angles. I understand that your head may be spinning by now as you become aware that pricing is a little more complex than you may have previously thought. But there's still more to come on pricing. In this chapter, I share with you some of my rules to help you to price effectively.

UNDERSTAND YOUR POSITION IN THE MARKET

Every business, regardless of whether it is a large and established business or a start-up business, has a position in the market place. Can you describe, in a few words, what your position or niche in the market is? Byronvale Advisors, for example, is a management consultant but its niche is, 'Recovery, Rebuild,

Restructure'. It also has a tagline of 'Turning Business Nightmares into Dreams'.

Being able to succinctly define your niche or position in the market gives you a foundation on which to base your pricing.

CALCULATE THE BENEFITS TO YOUR CUSTOMER OR CLIENT

The product you produce or the service you provide must have some inherent benefit to the customer or client. For your customer or client, the product or service will either make more money for them, save money for them or provide them with some other benefit that is non-monetary such as warmth, comfort, safety, etc.

Making money and saving money benefits can be calculated and used as a check to see if your pricing is competitive. Non-monetary benefits are harder to calculate but they will be compared to the benefits the products or services of your competitor can provide, e.g. warmer, closer, locally made, etc.

THINK ABOUT YOUR COMPETITION

Objectively look at your competition and determine how close your product or service is to that of the competition. The closer you are, the closer your pricing needs to be to the competition.

UNDERSTAND YOUR COSTS

In the previous chapter, we discussed the importance of fixed and variable costs in relation to the profitability building (or survival) objective. It is also important to understand your sunk costs, which are costs that have occurred in the past that can no longer be controlled or managed such as patents, the cost of incorporation, research and development, etc. It should also be noted that sunk costs should not be included in the pricing.

PRICE TO OPTIMISE PROFIT

As discussed previously, a buyer of your product or service pays the price they value your product or service at. The buyer does not consider your costs. The price should however always be greater than the minimum cost to provide your product or service.

REDUCING PRICES IS EASIER THAN INCREASING PRICES

Reducing and raising prices both contain an element of risk, however reducing prices is less risky than raising prices. Demand is likely to reduce faster if you raise prices rather than reduce prices. Price increases should only be looked at after your product or service has been in the market for a while and is established.

DOES YOUR PRICE MATCH YOUR BRAND?

Consider your brand and what that brand is trying to portray to the market. If your product or service is a discount or low-value brand then the price should reflect that. Conversely, if your product or service is prestigious or exclusive then the price should also reflect that.

NOTHING STAYS THE SAME – INCLUDING PRICE

Over time, the market and environment where you are selling your product or service changes. These changes affect your costs and the benefit or value they give your clients and customers. Therefore, they also must affect the price. Services can normally react faster to market and environmental changes than products such as retail or subscription products.

KEY POINT: The price you set for your products and services is one of the most crucial decisions you have to make in business.

CHAPTER 11

Understanding financial information and figures

Most people in business are great at what they do but when you talk to them about financial figures they run for the hills. There are some basic numbers and ratios every business owner just needs to know – and luckily, they are easy and quick.

So, let's start with a few. Don't worry, I'm not trying to make you into an accountant but I am trying to give you a basic understanding of the financial drivers of your business.

Firstly, though, a caveat – financial numbers should never be looked at in isolation. Either they should be compared to the industry benchmarks and/or should be analysed over time as a trend.

WHY DO YOU NEED TO KNOW THE NUMBERS?

The numbers, ratios and margins are important because they tell us whether your company is making an adequate return. An 'adequate' return is subjective – what is adequate to one person, one investor, one owner, one banker, or one industry may be different to what others consider adequate.

Companies offering a product or service that is easily replicated or commoditised usually have low margins. Companies that have a competitive advantage or a barrier to entry usually have high margins. New products usually have a high margin to begin with and as competition increases the margin reduces.

Let's take a look at profit margins first – the gross profit margin to be precise.

PROFITABILITY RATIOS

Gross profit margin

This ratio tells us how much of the revenue is left over after we have paid for the product that generated the revenue. You calculate it as follows:

> Gross profit margin = (revenue less cost of goods sold)/revenue
>
> e.g. 40% = ($1,000,000 – $600,000)/$1,000,000

In the example above, 40% of the revenue is left over after paying for the product.

This number is important (and arguably the most important) because it will quickly tell us if there is sufficient revenue left over to cover our selling and administrative costs or overheads.

Increasing sales or revenues alone without understanding and managing the costs will create cash flow problems and make your business unprofitable. Just looking at the gross profit margin will very quickly tell you if you are in a good position.

Operating profit margin

The operating profit margin tells you how much profit the business is generating after you have taken into account both the cost of goods sold and the operational and administrative expenses. It is calculated thus:

Operating profit margin = (gross profit less operating expenses)/revenue

e.g. 22.5% = ($400,000 − $175,000)/$1,000,000

For sole trader type businesses, I suggest that owner drawings – i.e. wages and expenses – are excluded from this calculation.

For example, if you run a café, excluding the owner-related expenses will give you a better picture of whether the café is generating enough revenue to cover its running or operating costs.

If, as an owner, you decide to pay yourself too much and your drawings are included in the operating costs, the picture the operating profit margin paints distorts the reality.

Operating profit margin is often confused with net profit margin.

Net profit margin

The net profit margin shows the profitability of the business after all costs. It also shows the return to the shareholder or owner and is calculated as follows:

Net profit margin = (net profit)/revenue

e.g. 7.5% = $75,000/$1,000,000

This ratio should be analysed over time and you are looking for a consistent and strong ratio. Deterioration of your net profit margin over time may indicate a period of abnormal costs or conditions. It may also indicate cost blow-outs.

Your net profit margin should be compared to the industry and/or the shareholder or owners' expectation of adequate return. A low margin compared to the industry average indicates a margin squeeze and is telling you that productivity improvements or initiatives are needed. A shareholder or business owner should expect a return that is representative of the risk of the investment.

QUICK DECISIONS USING PROFITABILITY NUMBERS

Your profit margins are a quick way of flagging problems. If you look at the profitability numbers and they are low, you can take some quick steps to improve the numbers. Here are some things you can do:

Increase revenue

'How do we do this?' I hear you cry. You are selling as much as you can and you can't afford the investment in more staff or materials, and even if you could you don't have the capacity! Or is it that it's just a competitive market place and you have to sell your product as cheaply as you can?

Well, how about increasing your prices by 2% every year? Cost pressures rise with inflation – the raw materials, fuel, etc., all rise by a small amount gradually. When they do, your profitability – gross margin – is getting squeezed.

Say you buy a coffee from your local café every morning on your way to work for $3.60. It's convenient and the coffee is good. One day you go to pay for your coffee and the price has increased to $3.70. You would most likely pay the $3.70 and continue your normal daily routine and continue paying $3.70, wouldn't you? This is a price increase of 2.78%.

These small increases either protect your gross profit margin or go directly to your overall profitability.

Think about it – how many customers would you be likely to lose? Customers that are so sensitive to such small increases are often customers that you are better off not retaining.

To minimise the impact of any price rises, you could try even smaller increases but make them more regularly – say quarterly. The impact on the customer may be even less noticeable.

Another way to look at this is:

- 2% increase = it's unlikely you would lose a customer
- 10% increase = would you lose less than 10% of your sales in dollars?
- 50% increase = would you lose less than 50% of your sales in dollars?

Reduce cost of goods sold

Reducing the cost of goods sold is a lot harder than increasing profit. This is because you are restrained by the variable components making up the cost of goods sold and the volume being produced and/or sold.

Apart from improving profitability, the process of looking at how you can reduce the cost of goods sold will give you a lot better understanding of the drivers, pain points, restrictions and opportunities in your business.

Below is a list of ideas for reducing your costs of goods sold. Maybe only a few will be applicable to your business, but even one idea that you can implement may contribute to reducing your cost of goods sold and therefore increasing your profit margin.

- *Source cheaper inputs or materials.* I worked with a steel manufacturing company and the supplier of a raw material would sometimes restrict supply to keep the average price higher. Not only did this affect certainty of supply but it also kept cost of goods sold high. My company turned around and sourced an alternative raw material from overseas, which in turn led to a joint-venture proposal.

- *Just in time purchasing – buy the materials when you need them.* The same steel company had an inventory policy whereby if they sold a particular item they would reorder the material immediately. While I was with the company, they sold steel for a wine vat and reordered the materials. They hadn't sold steel for a wine vat for the four years prior to my coming on board and they probably haven't since.

- *Buy in bulk.* Yes, I just said buy just in time, but if you have the capability and the working capital you may find buying in bulk will lower your per-unit input cost and the cost of goods sold.

- *Reduce waste.* Particularly if the cost of the raw material is high. Let's say you make granite benchtops and granite is a high cost material. If you can use exactly the right size material, you will minimise the waste and reduce your cost of goods sold.

- *Standardise product features.* Remember what Henry Ford said about the Model T Ford – you can have it in any colour as long as it's black. Reducing the options and non-standard features will reduce your costs.

- *Look at total cost.* The material cost is just one factor. Review funding costs, delivery costs or delivery time. Could you pay for the material quicker and get a more favourable price? Could you order earlier and reduce postage costs with slower delivery?

- *Team up with someone else.* Could you team up with someone else to avail yourself of a better price?

- *Get a long-term supply contract.* Byronvale Advisors discounts their hourly rate to clients who enter fixed price or retainer contracts. Apart from providing certainty of cash flows to Byronvale Advisors, it lowers the price to the client and it also provides the client price certainty.

KEY POINT: Your key profit numbers can sound alarm bells that make you implement changes to stay in business!

KEY POINT

Activity ratios

Activity ratios tell you how efficiently your business is using its short-term assets, especially cash. They indicate your operational performance. Let's take a look at the main activity ratios in this chapter. If you don't understand activity ratios, you risk a deterioration in your business' performance and ultimately your business could fail.

WORKING CAPITAL (CURRENT RATIO)

The working capital ratio can give you an indication of the ability of your business to pay its bills. You calculate it using the following equation:

Working capital ratio = (current assets)/(current liabilities)

e.g. $2.27 = \$250,000/\$110,000$

A strong working capital ratio (any number higher than 2) indicates a better ability to meet ongoing and unexpected bills, therefore taking the pressure off your cash flow. If you are in a 'liquid' position, with plenty of cash in the business, you have other advantages such as being able to negotiate cash discounts with your suppliers.

A weaker working capital ratio may indicate that your business is having greater difficulties meeting its short-term commitments. In other words, you're finding it tough paying the bills – so additional working capital support is required.

Having to pay bills before payments are received may be an issue that a short-term overdraft facility could assist with. Alternatively, building up a reserve of cash investments may create a sound working capital buffer.

Your net working capital can also be used to estimate the ability of your company to grow quickly.

If your business has substantial cash reserves, it may have enough cash to rapidly scale up the business. Conversely, a tight working capital situation makes it quite unlikely that a business has the financial means to accelerate its rate of growth.

A working capital ratio greater than 2 is usually considered desirable; however, it is a matter of balance.

DEBTOR DAYS

Debtor days are a measure of the average length of time it takes from when you make a sale to when you receive payment. This number measures how quickly and efficiently you are collecting your outstanding bills.

A larger number of debtor days means that your business must invest more cash in its unpaid accounts receivable asset, while a smaller number implies that there is a smaller investment in accounts receivable, therefore more cash is available for other uses.

You calculate your debtor days as follows:

Debtor days = (average debtors)/(annual revenue) multiplied by 365

e.g. 38 days = $105,000/$1,000,000 x 365

Debtor days should be looked at over time to see if there is a trend. A long number of debtor days may indicate that customers are struggling to pay their accounts. Or it could just mean that you are slack when it comes to chasing payment. Also, economic factors such as a recession may lengthen debtor days and may require you to tighten your credit control processes.

Generally, lower debtor day numbers are better. However, a low debtor day number compared to the industry benchmark may mean your credit terms are too stringent and that you are potentially missing out on sales opportunities.

It is also a useful exercise to list your debtors and then order them by how outstanding their debts are. This is known as an aged debtor report.

An aged debtor report divides the age of the accounts receivable into various categories, which you can sometimes alter within the accounting software to match your billing terms.

The most common time categories are from 0 to 30 days old, 31 to 60 days old, 61 to 90 days old and older than 90 days. Any invoices falling into the time category representing periods greater than 30 days are cause for an increasing sense of alarm, especially if they drop into the oldest time category.

Your aged debtor report prioritises the debtors that need following up, and accounting software systems will also often provide the contact name, email address and phone number of who you need to chase for payment, to bring their account into line.

CREDITOR DAYS

Creditor days indicate the average length of time it takes your business to pay its bills. Here's how you calculate your creditor days:

Creditor days = (average trade creditors)/(annual revenue) multiplied by 365

e.g. 60 days = $165,000/$1,000,000 x 365

Again, this ratio needs to look at a trend and be compared to industry benchmarks. A declining ratio may indicate you have a worsening working capital position. This could be due to a decreasing stock turn or lengthening number of debtor days.

If you are finding it more difficult to pay your bills on time, as well as being a red flag for other problems in the business, it will put your creditors offside. They won't like waiting for payment because it blows out their debtor days!

The last thing you want is for your creditors to stop extending you credit which will further worsen your cash flow position.

INVENTORY DAYS OR STOCK TURN

The inventory days or stock turn number shows how many days it takes for your inventory to be sold and replaced. You calculate this as follows:

Inventory days = (average inventory)/(cost of goods sold) multiplied by 365

e.g. 61 days = $100,000/$600,000 x 365

For service-based businesses, you can replace average inventory with average work in progress.

A low inventory days measure may indicate positive factors such as good stock demand and management. It also means fewer resources (usually cash) are tied up in inventory. However, if your number of inventory days is too low, it may be a sign that the inventory levels are too low and you will be unable to support an increase in demand.

A high number of inventory days may indicate that either stock is naturally slow-moving or you have problems with your stock – much of it could be obsolete stock or it is getting damaged sitting in your warehouse for too long. A high inventory days number can also raise stock valuation issues. The inventory accounting standard requires you to write your stock value down, however most private companies are not required to produce accounts and do not write the inventory value down, which leads to a distortion of the inventory turn number.

Just be a bit cautious with the inventory days measure as it is very industry specific. In an industry where the inventory is not perishable or won't go out of date, it may be appropriate to have higher inventory days. Likewise, where the goods are imported and it takes time to replace inventory it may be appropriate to hold more inventory. This would be the case for a car sales business.

QUICK DECISIONS USING ACTIVITY NUMBERS

Activity numbers tell the business owner how efficiently they are using their short-term assets, especially cash. Having lots of capital tied up in inventory and debtors means the business has to find the cash to pay for them from somewhere – either through its own reserves, borrowings or by delaying paying creditors.

What is optimal depends on the industry and the products being sold, but as a generalisation:

- Debtor days need to be less than creditor days – have your customers paying you before you have to pay your suppliers. In the example above, debtor days were 38 days and creditor days were 60 days, which meant customers were paying quicker than the business needed to pay the suppliers.

- Inventory days should be less than creditor days – you are selling the inventory before you have to pay for it. In the example above, inventory days were 61 days and creditor days were 60 days – inventory is being sold about as quickly as the suppliers are being paid for it.

With inventory, there are a few common factors to be mindful of. Let's take a look at these.

First, the accounting method you use to value your stock can impact the overall valuation of your inventory. Second, obsolescent or hardcore inventory can impact the inventory valuation and days. Accounting standards have rules around writing the valuation of obsolescent inventory down.

Buying inventory at a discount can impact inventory days positively and negatively. Usually the trade-off for the discount is that you have to purchase in bulk. There is a balance between the value of the discount and the cost to fund the increase in inventory.

Discounting sales can also positively and negatively impact working capital. Offering customers a discount may increase the sales and/or decrease debtor days. If the discount increases the sales but does not decrease debtor days then consider the impact on working capital and cost of funds. Likewise, if the discount reduces debtor days but does not increase volume what is the impact on gross margin and profitability?

Chasing debtors is never fun – but remember the debtor amount is your money that someone else has. Would you be comfortable lending the customer the same value in cash if you had just been to the bank and withdrawn it from your bank account? It makes a big difference to your bank balance if they pay you.

Chasing debtors is never fun – but remember the debtor amount is your money that someone else has.

I have only ever had one client that turned into a bad debt. It was when I had sent several reminders and finally threatened legal action that they put themselves into voluntary liquidation. During this period, my wife had been saying I should not be pursuing the client and threatening legal action but my rhetorical question to her was, 'if the client walked into our house, found my wife's purse and took all the cash out of it, put it in their pocket and walked out the door what would you do?'

You need to invest the time to ensure you are paid in a timely manner and pursue late payers.

KEY POINT: If you don't know your activity ratios, you won't know if you are managing your cash flow as best you can.

CHAPTER 13

Liquidity ratios

The next set of numbers you need to understand to ensure your business is successful are liquidity ratios. These measure your business' ability to meet its short-term liabilities. In other words, they make sure you can pay your bills.

They are especially important to banks and creditors. You need to know your liquidity ratios are sound when you are applying for loans, and lenders will need to know them before they give you credit.

Let's take a look at some liquidity ratios.

CURRENT RATIO

The current ratio is also known as the working capital ratio, which we discussed in Chapter 12. It indicates if the business can pay off its short-term liabilities in an emergency by liquidating its current assets.

A high current ratio indicates a good level of liquidity, but if the ratio is too high it may indicate other problems. The inventory levels may be too high, or valued incorrectly, or include too much obsolete stock. There may also be a high debtor balance due to poor credit control or payment terms that are too generous.

QUICK ASSET RATIO

The quick asset ratio gives a more conservative measure of liquidity than the current ratio. This is because the quick asset ratio excludes inventory. It regards the value of the inventory as a lot less than its book value if it has to be realised in a 'fire sale' situation. It should also exclude any prepaid expenses. It is calculated as follows:

Quick asset ratio = (current assets less inventory and prepaid expenses)/(current liabilities)

e.g. 1.27 = ($250,000 − $100,000 − $10,000)/$110,000

In the example above, the business' quick asset ratio is greater than 1, which indicates that current liabilities can be met from the current assets without having to sell any stock in a hurry.

CASH RATIO

The cash ratio is like the quick asset ratio but it excludes any other non-cash current assets such as debtors. It is the most conservative liquidity ratio. Here's how you calculate it:

Cash ratio = (cash balances)/(current liabilities)

e.g. 0.09 = $10,000/$110,000

USING LIQUIDITY NUMBERS

A caveat to liquidity ratios is that the ratio is just the start of the conversation. Ratios do need to be benchmarked against similar businesses and over a period of time.

After you have determined the ratio, you also need to analyse the make-up and timing of the liabilities. Let's take a look at an example.

A not-for-profit client had a balance sheet that looked a bit like this:

Current Assets

Cash	$20,000
Prepaid expenses	$60,000
Total current assets	$80,000

Current liabilities

GST	$2,400
Income in advance	$21,750
Provision for prize money	$7,500
Provision for grants	$6,200
Trade and other payables	$32,300
Total current liabilities	$70,150

Current ratio = 1.14
Quick asset ratio = 0.29
Cash ratio = 0.29

A quick glance would indicate that this organisation can pay its short-term liabilities by liquidating its short-term assets. However, by looking at the quick asset and cash ratios you could see that it could only cover 29% of its current liabilities if it had to liquidate its assets quickly, and this would not even cover the trade payables.

The quick asset and cash ratios, however, do not look at the timings of the current liabilities in the calculation.

In the above example, in a 'fire sale' situation, the income in advance contractually would not need to be paid. The prize money provision was also payable towards the end of the 12-month period.

The major creditor in the trade payables has, over a period of time, demonstrated they were lenient on enforcing payment terms. So, if I were to adjust the quick asset ratio and cash ratio to reflect only the items that are immediately payable, the ratio would be 2.33 or 233%. With the timing adjusted, the quick asset ratio would indicate this organisation had a strong liquidity position at that point in time.

So, liquidity ratios are very useful, but require a little more skill in interpretation.

KEY POINT: Businesses can suffer greatly due to poor cash flow management. The ratios explained in this chapter will help you keep track of whether you have enough cash to pay the bills!

PART 4

Marketing
and sales

CHAPTER 14

New world marketing

The world is changing at lightning speed and the way we conduct business is also changing at lightning speed. I'm in my mid-forties and I can remember when scientific calculators were first allowed in schools and exams, and we used punch cards to program a computer that filled an entire room.

Likewise, in our businesses, the way we market and sell has also evolved.

Traditional marketing – making cold calls, placing large print media advertisements and interruptive advertisements on TV – was all about the company finding the customer. These marketing techniques were interruptive and became ineffective as their target audience used technology such as caller ID, video recording and spam filters to avoid the message. These techniques are also expensive types of marketing. The marketer-centric style is convenient for the marketer as they can push out the content to people – potential customers – regardless of whether they want it or not. But it's not a great start to attract a potential customer.

Today, we flip the traditional marketing model on its head. Instead of pushing content out to potential customers, we try to attract and empower customers to find us. It is customer-focused and about fulfilling a customer's needs rather than the company's needs.

The customer has all the power. They don't call a salesperson – instead, they jump online and research the product or service and often purchase online too.

Marketing, and specifically inbound marketing, is about drawing people in – hence the 'in' in inbound – and creating marketing that people love, and the customer being part of the conversation.

INBOUND MARKETING

Inbound marketing is about being found by customers. It is focused on the customer's needs and earning the customer's trust. As noted above, it is not like traditional marketing which is about buying the customer's attention through newspaper and TV advertisements and other promotional material.

To quote Wikipedia:

> 'Inbound marketing provides *information*, an improved *customer experience* and builds *trust* by offering potential customers information they value via company sponsored newsletters, blogs and entries on social media platforms.'

The key words in this definition are italicised, and I'll repeat them here:

- Information
- Customer experience
- Trust.

Below is a useful diagram courtesy of HubSpot that outlines a simple inbound marketing methodology.

Inbound methodology

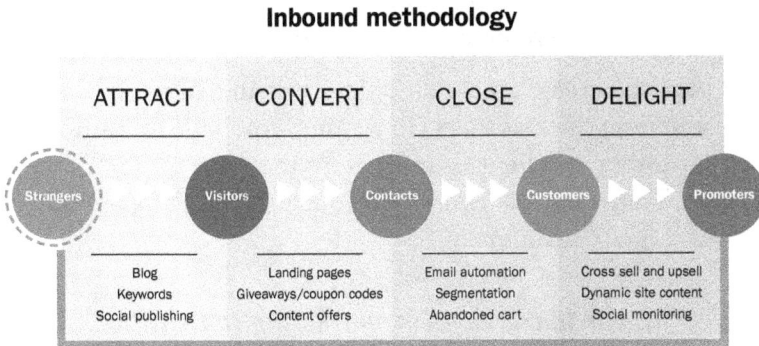

ATTRACT	CONVERT	CLOSE	DELIGHT
Strangers → Visitors	Contacts	Customers	Promoters
Blog	Landing pages	Email automation	Cross sell and upsell
Keywords	Giveaways/coupon codes	Segmentation	Dynamic site content
Social publishing	Content offers	Abandoned cart	Social monitoring

Source: HubSpot offers free Inbound Certification courses online at https://academy.hubspot.com/certification

The diagram summarises how inbound marketing works:

1. First, you need to 'attract' strangers to become visitors

2. Then you convert them into potential customers

3. Next, close the sale and make them actual customers

4. Finally, delight them so they become promoters of your business.

Along the bottom of the diagram are some of the tools to use at the different stages.

What I think this process overlooks is the important step of 'analysis'. As a marketer, you need to understand what is working and what is not and then the marketing needs to be refined and adapted to be more effective and efficient.

TARGET PERSONAS

A large part of inbound marketing is about providing content and information to your visitor, lead or customer. Let's look now at some content creation best practices.

Your aim is to create great marketing content to attract, convert, close and delight customers. To do this, you have to know who your customer or client is and where they are on the buyer's journey. That way you can make your marketing very specific to your target customers.

> *Your aim is to create great marketing content to attract, convert, close and delight customers.*

Do you know who your customers or clients are? Who are you trying to attract, convert, close and delight? What are your prospects' personas?

Personas are representations of your business' ideal customers that you create to help your team develop focused content and nurturing strategies. Personas are the person your marketing is trying to reach. Don't misunderstand personas as customer segmentation. Personas are a lot deeper – they reveal attitudes, ideals and the thoughts of that persona.

I love the Youi insurance TV advertisements – they communicate that Youi has a firm idea of their personas and therefore have a good understanding of their customers and what they want. You should be able to find them on YouTube as an example. To get an idea of what a persona looks like, here are some examples:

> 'Hi, I'm Stephen, 40+ year old, expat kiwi, married with two daughters who owns a small management consulting business in Melbourne, who loves fly fishing.'

'Hi, I'm Eliza and I'm in my last year at teacher's college. I live at home with my parents and intend to travel overseas in the middle of next year – and my boyfriend will probably stay behind as he is finishing his apprenticeship.'

UNDERSTANDING YOUR BUYER'S JOURNEY

Once you have an understanding of who you are targeting your marketing to, you need to work out the steps your customers go through before they make a purchase. This is often referred to as the buyer's journey. Many companies will attempt to 'map' this journey.

The buyer's journey map is made up of three stages:

1. Awareness;

2. Consideration; and

3. Decision.

It is important that you know where your customer/buyer is on the journey map because it can help you refine your content marketing to each persona.

Your content may focus on the problem your buyer persona is experiencing, then that would be an awareness stage piece of content. If your content is more about the solution to a problem, then it would be focused on the consideration stage. As for the decision stage, that's when you begin to create content about your product or service.

Let's take a look at these three stages in more detail.

Awareness

The awareness stage is the stage when your prospect or potential customer begins their research online to figure out what their problem or need is. It is the stage where they 'don't know what they don't know'.

Most potential customers and clients research online nowadays and 70% of people use Google. Expert content, whitepapers, analyst reports, blog posts, research reports, eBooks, videos, editorial content and educational content are examples of 'content assets' at the awareness stage.

When a prospect is experiencing and expressing symptoms of a problem or opportunity, these 'content assets' help educate or inform your buyer persona.

It is important that this content focuses just on your buyer persona's need, problem or pain point, and not on a solution – you are educating and not selling.

Content that educates or informs will draw those target personas in the awareness stage to your website. As your prospect gets further into their research, they will begin to understand which criteria do and do not meet their needs. This allows them to prioritise their questions.

At this point, buyers can begin to eliminate vendors that don't provide the functionality or service that they're looking for. They can narrow down their focus to just a few competing companies.

Your awareness content – in fact, any of your content – does not just have to be written, it can be visual and audio too.

Bunnings and Mitre 10 hardware stores have DIY videos – how to mix concrete, how to build a table, etc. You don't have to be a Bunnings or Mitre 10 customer to benefit from this content and next time you're purchasing hardware, you might just consider Bunnings or Mitre 10 for their know-how and generosity.

So, going back to the Wikipedia definition of inbound marketing – you are providing information.

Consideration

In the consideration stage, the prospect has clearly defined and given a name to their problem or opportunity. For example, they know their house is not safe from robbers and they need a security system installed.

The 'content assets' in this stage should speak directly to the solutions that can help solve their needs. Here you are bridging the gap between educational assets and product or service information without involving your brand. That's why expert guides such as live interactions, webcasts, podcasts, videos and comparison whitepapers work so well for this stage.

Going back to our example, the persona may be a homeowner whose house was robbed. The content marketing may be in the form of a video about mobile security technology. The message to the prospect might be to watch this video and see how you can use mobile technology that can be paired to a home alarm system. Why do you add this? Because by going into further detail on the product, and outlining some of the nifty things you can do with this technology, you're giving them some extra information to think about.

A real example of this type of content marketing is ring.com's wireless doorbells video. This is the customer experience part of inbound marketing.

Decision

The prospect at the decision stage has decided on their solution strategy, method or approach and is making a decision. It may have taken the prospect days, weeks or even months of education and research to arrive at this stage. They are now ready to make a purchase (now that they know about their problem and have determined an ideal solution), so it's time to show why you're the best of the best.

This is the trust part of inbound marketing. Your content here will be focused on your own product and service. You may decide to use formats such as vendor or product comparisons, case studies, trial downloads, product literature, testimonials and live demos – it's also the bragging stage.

Even after your buyers have made a purchase, their work isn't over. Most buyers will continue to research best practices, implementation guides and more, to make sure they're ready to hit the ground running with their new purchase. You might want to consider a program of marketing to the customer such as advanced product features or tips for using the product safely so when they want to renew or upgrade they feel continually looked after.

KEY POINT: It is important that you know where your customer/buyer is on the journey map because it can help you refine your content marketing to each persona.

CHAPTER 15

It's all about the content

You're probably realising that new marketing hinges on content, which is what we're going to concentrate on here. Businesses that fail to adopt content-based marketing, tailored to their particular industry, will struggle. Old marketing does not work – at least it won't continue to work for much longer.

A very useful way of putting all your new world marketing together is to create a content map that details the content for each persona at each stage of the customer journey. A content map gives you guidance and helps with planning the direction of the content you produce rather than throwing darts in the dark.

Yes, it's really just another a plan!

CREATING YOUR CONTENT

Next you need to get on and create the content. The content doesn't have to be lengthy or elaborate, in fact YouTube videos work better when they don't look as if they were made by professionals on state-of-the art equipment. However, you are trying to create remarkable content and not just numerous content.

Here are some tips for creating engaging content:

- Create content for the persona *and* where they are on the journey map.

- The more specific your content, the better. Yes, broad content can cast a wider net, but specific content is going to attract qualified visitors and leads – those who are more likely to become customers. This also means you need to understand your competitive advantage (see the strategic planning process in Chapters 5 and 6 of this book).

- Less is more. Your personas are probably just as busy as you are so make it easy for them to consume your content. Don't go creating 30-minute videos and 100 page eBooks. Focus more on covering the topic in full in an easily digestible way rather than creating a lengthy piece of content.

- Keep the content educational and informative, not promotional. It's not until the decision stage of the buyer's journey that your product should be mentioned.

- Design is secondary. Focus on the informational part of the content first by writing great content rather than making that content look nice and pretty.

- Seek out help. If writing and producing other types of content doesn't come easily to you and you don't have time (after all, you're running a business!) then there are people out there who will help you. Jump online and find them. Notice as you do so your journey, the content you're reading in your research and how you respond.

So, now you've developed your customer personas, you know where they are on the journey map, you've put a content plan together and developed a suite of content. Next, you have to figure out how to get the content out to your customers and prospects.

PROMOTING YOUR CONTENT

Have you ever published something on a blog or on social media and wondered why you never had a comment, like or retweet? You can't just expect people to find your content – you have to promote it.

The right distribution technique gets the right content in front of the right person at the right time. There are several ways to promote your content. Here are a few ideas:

- *Website pages and business blogs.* These are not only for content, but also for hosting the different content offers that you have created. Landing pages will act as the gatekeeper for your extensive range of content offers.

- *Calls to action.* These can be placed on your website to entice your website visitors to download or request your different offers.

- *Email.* You can use email to let your prospects know about the exciting new pieces of content you've created.

- *Social media.* Keep your buyer persona in mind when using social media to communicate messages about your products or services. Different demographics use different social media platforms to find this type of information. Many Baby Boomers and older people are less likely to use social media. Millennials are more likely to search for products or services on social media rather than using websites, and Gen X typically use all online platforms, although more discerningly. (We discuss social media in the next chapter.)

- *Optimise your webpages.* Ensure that you maximise your website's search engine optimisation (SEO) potential and utilise keywords in your content and webpages. Pick a few keywords that reflect what you do or sell and incorporate them into all of your content and webpages.

You need to be promoting your content constantly. There is no point only writing a blog post once every six months or tweeting twice a year. There are tools that can assist with scheduling content promotion (see Chapter 16 on social media).

You can also re-promote content. An eBook that was promoted six months ago can be promoted again (assuming the content is still relevant). A tweet that was posted last week can be posted again another week. An email that was sent to one group last week could be sent to another group this week. At least as much time needs to go into promoting the content as creating the content.

ANALYSING YOUR CONTENT

You might find that even with all this content it's much harder to capture the attention of your prospect. Remember, it's an issue of fighting for attention rather than space. People have limited attention spans, so you need remarkable content to reel them in. That content needs to be shared with the world in a way that helps you achieve your business goals.

Marketing, and in particular inbound marketing, is about delivering something to the customer that appeals to them and it has to be something that they need. It is no longer a case of 'we'll make it because we know what our customer wants, and we know our customer better than they know themselves'.

Marketing, and in particular inbound marketing, is about delivering something to the customer that appeals to them.

You need to analyse your content's efficacy in order to get the most out of it. Are you creating content on the right topics? Is it in the correct formats? Is it being distributed in the right ways?

Make sure what you're doing is working and find out why it worked or why it didn't. Use that insight to create better content moving forward.

You can use the following metrics when you are analysing content:

- *Number of visits.* How many views did your content have?

- *Leads generated.* Did your content offer convert leads? How many? Did it reach your goal?

- *Social shareability.* Did anyone share your content on social media? How many times? Is it getting re-tweeted or re-posted?

- *Inbound links.* Are there any outside websites linking to your content? This could help build authority to your website and your content.

- *Content performance by author.* Is one author/creator's content performing better than another? Should they be creating the majority of content in the future? Or are there certain tips they follow that are worth sharing with your other content creators?

- *Content performance by topic.* Do your buyer personas prefer a certain topic that you're covering? If so, continue writing about that content!

- *Content performance by format.* Is there a certain format that is performing better than another? This can also give you insights on your personas. If they don't seem to be coming to your webinars, maybe that's not the right content for your persona and you should test something else out.

It's important to go through the whole process – from developing personas, creating content, distribution and analysis – and as Jason Squires from Social Pipeline Marketing says 'rinse and repeat'. Take what you have learned from each piece of content to help create more effective content down the road. Continue repeating this content process and learning more about the content your buyer personas consider remarkable. It's not a set and forget exercise.

Let's look at a case study now to illustrate our discussion on inbound marketing.

Inbound marketing case study

A couple of years ago, Byronvale Advisors was engaged to assist a not-for-profit organisation whose membership numbers were falling. Byronvale Advisors contracted customer experience consultants to work with them on this problem for the client.

The first thing we did was get an understanding of the organisation's mission (see Chapters 5 and 6 for more about strategic planning). This gave us an understanding of the organisation's core purpose – why it existed – but more importantly, why the board and C-suite thought the organisation existed.

We then conducted a series of quick tele-interviews with a range of stakeholders – members, board directors, advisers – young and old, city and country, Australian and international. This was formulating the value propositions that each member wanted from the organisation.

Next, we held a workshop with the board and C-suite and during that workshop we started building personas.

Persona # 1: Jane works in Bega (country NSW) at a manufacturing company. She is married with two primary-school-aged girls. Spending time with the family is important for Jane and she values the country lifestyle, although she relishes her annual girls' weekend in the 'big smoke'. The company Jane works for is small and Jane covers a broad range of tasks. She has two staff reporting to her. Because of the location and the small team covering a broad range of tasks the training needs to be online via webinars, etc., and also short and has to cover broad issues.

Persona # 2: John is in his late fifties and lives in Sydney. John is divorced and has two adult sons (and is hoping for some grandchildren). John is a C-suite executive in an ASX20 company. Every summer he crews on a yacht in the Sydney to Hobart Race. John likes conferences and half-day seminars as, apart from the education they provide, he values the opportunity to network.

We developed five personas in total.

The next stage of building the membership proposition was to develop a suite of products and services for each member persona – webinars, networking functions, seminar-lite products, a training and information hub, eMagazines, etc.

We then started to develop an inbound marketing plan to target each persona. This included social media, redeveloping the website, creating landing pages and calls-to-action, implementing a customer relationship management (CRM) system so we could analyse the contact that members had with the organisation and target members based on that interaction.

The point is, we didn't just sit back and say, 'Let's run a conference' and hope that the content, speakers, location and timing that suited us would attract people to the conference. If we were going to run a conference, we had to know exactly who it was targeting, what they wanted, how they wanted it, where and when they wanted it. We also needed to know how to connect with that target market. We developed a plan to attract, convert, close and delight – then we analysed, rinsed and repeated.

KEY POINT: New marketing hinges on content that provides information to the buyer in a way and format that the buyer relates to.

CHAPTER 16

Social media

There is a range of social media platforms – Twitter, Facebook, LinkedIn, Instagram, Pinterest, Google+, Blab and the list goes on... and on... and on. So, which social media platform should you be using in your marketing and why?

As a rule of thumb, there are only three that I would use:

- Twitter
- Facebook
- LinkedIn.

To refine this further, if you're a business to consumer (B2C) business then I would recommend just focusing on Twitter and Facebook. If you're a business to business (B2B) business then I would just use Twitter and LinkedIn.

FACEBOOK

Mark Zuckerberg started Facebook for his fellow students out of his dorm room at Harvard. Today, every man and his dog (yes – my sister-in-law's dog has a Facebook page) can be found on Facebook.

Facebook, as a marketing tool for your business, has the following strengths and weaknesses:

Strengths. Facebook is widely-adopted by large segments of the population. It can be used to market to your target customer and you can narrow the intended audience down to target the exact persona.

Weaknesses. It is reasonably time-consuming, requires monitoring as it is easy for people to vent, write false allegations, or spam your business page.

LINKEDIN

This is the granddaddy of them all. LinkedIn has been around since 2003, which, in social media terms is also known as 'the beginning of time'.

LinkedIn has both strengths and weaknesses for businesses:

Strengths. Everybody who is anybody is on LinkedIn.

Weaknesses. Most people have trouble knowing what to do with LinkedIn after they upload their business information. LinkedIn company pages are not very useful – you are better to use a personal page that is adapted for your business. For example, see Bryonvale Advisors on LinkedIn: https://www.linkedin.com/in/byronvaleadvisors/

TWITTER

Twitter is a surprisingly successful tool (just ask Donald Trump) that has been widely adopted and used for everything from business to fun and games. It has the following strengths and weaknesses:

Strengths. It is used by large segments of the population. By using apps such as ManageFlitter, you can build a target audience and spy on your competition.

Weaknesses. It can be a distraction, especially if you have attention deficit disor... wow, look at that bird outside my window!

Social media is just another form of content marketing, so why do some people find it scary? Maybe it's because they don't understand the markets that use different social media platforms. Or maybe it's because they think all anyone does is 'play and waste time' on social media (my wife who is a doctor calls it an i-disorder). Or maybe it's because they feel that it is a total distraction from doing 'real work' or 'real marketing'.

Social media, however, is part of a marketing content plan, which should include a social media strategy and plan.

So, what do you need to do?

1. Develop a social media strategy similar to a business-wide strategic plan.

2. Have a planning calendar. Each week put down the idea or topic for social media marketing for your business. Then allocate your ideas for each week by social media platform – which idea will be better executed via a tweet, Facebook or LinkedIn post?

3. Start collating the social media marketing.

4. Schedule the tweets and posts using a social media scheduling app such as Hootsuite or Statusbrew. I have tweets and posts scheduled for weeks in advance. So even when I'm fly fishing and nowhere near a computer or internet access, I'm active on a social media.

5. Once a day, spend no more than 30 minutes checking activity on social media, contribute to the activity of your target market, interact with 'centres of influence' or those people who can boost your market credibility and access.

6. Once a week, spend time on content creation and reviewing your competitors – for no more than an hour!

7. Once a month, plan monetisation campaigns using social media – competitions, special offers, referrals or campaigns for future leads or prospects.

8. Once a month, analyse your social media strategy and monitor the success of the strategy and/or campaign to date.

HOW TO GET FREE MARKETING AND MEDIA EXPOSURE

Even with the best inbound and social media marketing strategy, there is still the need to up the ante to get your message out there. To do this you can revert to mainstream or conventional types of media – TV, radio, newspapers and magazines.

However, most small businesses avoid publicity and/or avoid using a public relations (PR) firm because they think it is really expensive, and the result is not something that is tangible or measurable up front. They regard it as an expensive leap of faith. They might also feel that PR is just about brand awareness – which it is – but it is also about getting 'bums on seats' – getting people to buy your product or service. So, publicity equals profit.

How do you get media exposure – preferably for free?

Firstly, don't wait for the perfect time to publicise your business ('I'll wait until we are a bit more established, or until the new packaging is out, or wait until…') – there is no perfect time.

Next, build on the knowledge you have about your customer or client personas and then try to think where they would hang out.

I have done some work with a vision impairment disability organisation. Most people with a vision impairment start losing their vision later in life. So I contacted *The Senior* newspaper that is aimed directly at senior citizens, and I got an article published in that newspaper.

Younger people might hang out in online forums. Look at the explosion of blogs for mothers over the last few years.

Next, create a media release (also known as a press release). The media release has several standard sections to it:

- *Headline.* This is straight to the point and sums up the story.
- *Opening line.* A very brief overview of the story.
- *Text.* This should be written in the third person with lots of quotes – the who, what, where, how, why and when.
- *Format.* It needs to look like a media release – with a heading on the page saying 'Media Release'.
- *Contact details.* Give all of them: email, phone, website, Twitter, LinkedIn, Facebook, etc.

When sending the media release, do not attach the media release but incorporate it into the body of the email. Attachments get stopped at firewalls and people (journalists) have to take another step to open the attachment to read it. They can only read the headline and opening line in the body of the email via preview modes.

Never make an announcement in a media release. By that I mean something along the lines of 'Stephen is pleased to announce the publication of his first book…'. Instead, the media release should pique the interest of whoever is receiving it, e.g. 'The only reasons to be in business'.

After you have created and sent your media release, make sure you follow up with a phone call. Given you have done your research on where in the media your target audience hang out, you might only have a dozen outlets that you have sent your media release to. You will also need to be aware of when the publications go out, e.g. is it a monthly newspaper at the start of the month, or is it breakfast TV?

Time your follow-up phone call with the journalist's deadlines in mind. Make sure also that the journalist has had the opportunity to read your media release. Before you actually pick up the phone and call, prepare for the phone call. Prepare for questions they may ask you and then prepare your response to those questions.

KEY POINT: Once you have sent out your press release, always follow up with a phone call.

CHAPTER 17

Inbound sales

Like inbound marketing, inbound sales is a change of focus about how we sell to customers. With your potential customers now having the power to research products and services around their personal needs, there is a change from seller-centric selling to buyer-centric selling.

Inbound sales is focused on the individual customer's needs, their pain points, frustrations and goals. Inbound sales is about helping the customer and not about closing a sale.

Now that you have created the leads through inbound marketing, you need to convert those leads into sales to monetise them.

Inbound marketing is about educating and providing information to potential customers. Inbound sales is about giving customers a relevant, personal, delightful experience, driven by their needs and on their timeline. (Again, notice the key concepts – information and customer experience.)

Did you know that by the time a potential customer is talking to a sales rep they have made around 60% of their purchase decision? Gone are the days of cold calls using a static sales pitch, nowadays the sales rep will tailor the sales pitch based on the buyer's particular situation and needs.

HubSpot's co-founder and CEO, Brian Halligan, says:

> 'Buyers have more information available to them and higher expectations for a relevant, personal experience when making a purchase. Giving them a relevant, personal, 'delightful' experience, driven by their needs, on their timeline is what an inbound approach to sales is all about.'

FROM SELLER-CENTRIC SELLING TO BUYER-CENTRIC SELLING

So how do you transform from seller-centric selling to buyer-centric selling? There are four key steps:

1. Transform the way you *target* accounts

2. Transform the way you *prospect* accounts

3. Transform the way you *connect* with accounts

4. Transform the way your prospects *perceive* you as a salesperson.

We'll take a look at each step in turn.

Transform the way you target accounts

With a bit of luck (no, actually, not luck, with a bit of good management) your inbound marketing will have targeted the information based on the buyer personas, and where those buyers are on the buyer journey map, so that the leads that enter the sales process are qualified leads and a good fit for your business.

Transform the way you prospect accounts

Blind or cold calling is very seller-centric. With inbound marketing and sales, remember that information is key. You need to be providing information to prospects and, likewise with inbound sales, educating yourself on your buyer prospect.

If you're a B2B firm then this might mean educating yourself on the target client or customer. For example, company size, annual revenue, what they sell and to whom, the person who you will be talking to, their role and who the decision-makers are. Has the company been in the media? Are they running an event? Do they have a new TV ad? Use social media to observe what your target customer or client posts and how they interact on social media.

As part of this information gathering, make sure you know how your sales target has interacted with your company. What have they downloaded? What pages did they look at on your website? How long did they spend on each page? This allows you to tailor the conversation to each lead.

You need to be not only knowledgeable about the product, as is the case with seller-centric selling, but also knowledgeable about the lead. There are a number of programs, apps and extensions that can be used to gather this information so it is on-hand as you are communicating with your sales target.

This information can also determine the purpose of the call. Is it just introductory? Is it to get referred to the decision-maker? Or is that call made to the decision-maker?

Transform the way you connect with accounts

You are now ready to pick up the phone and connect with your lead. There are four guidelines you want to follow when you do this:

1. *Build rapport.* Use the information you have gathered to get on the 'same page' as your prospect. Understand them. What keeps them awake at night? Build trust and rapport so they are comfortable talking to you. Remember, though, that you are educating and not selling. It's about the experience and not the process. I bought a car and I can tell people about my *experience*, but I've forgotten the process. (Note I have highlighted the key word again.)

2. *Know your audience.* The person who is the ultimate decision-maker is not usually the person you are going to end up talking with. Tailor the conversation to the person you're actually talking to and what they care about.

3. *Speak the prospect's language.* The way you talk and present information needs to resonate with the prospect. This is your opportunity to build credibility as being someone who knows about their industry.

4. *Be helpful.* Put together some information that can educate the person you talk to. Have a tip, an educational offer or other content to give to the prospect.

Transform the way your prospects perceive you as a salesperson

One of the key differences between seller-centric and buyer-centric sales is where the perceived power lies.

With seller-centric selling, the salesperson has all the information and perceived power. The reverse is true in a buyer-centric salesperson. You don't want to be a sales bully but rather a sales educator. You want the experience to delight. You want your prospects to feel comfortable with you and trust you.

You also want to humanise your company. This is very important because people buy from people.

The buyer doesn't want a robotic hard sales pitch, but they want to be listened to and understood. The sales pitch needs to address their personal needs.

When I ring my health insurer or bank, I'm told who I'm talking to. I'm asked if they can call me by my first name, and they might comment about the weather, or the latest round in the footy.

Become the trusted adviser. Walk in the prospect's shoes and understand their perspective. Through mutual understanding, trust is developed and people buy from people they trust.

Become the trusted adviser. Walk in the prospect's shoes and understand their perspective.

KEY POINT: Today's prospects respond to buyer-centric selling, which businesses must understand to offer an experience worth remembering that informs the buyer and develops mutual trust.

PART 5

Minimising your risk

CHAPTER 18

Only fools start a business with borrowed funds

In this last part of the book, I want to outline ways that you can run your business better from the outset. The first step is not to start your business venture with borrowed funds. Only an idiot borrows money or raises capital to start a new business!

Did that heading grab your attention? Good! This is really important. There is a time and a place for everything, and I'm not saying never borrow money. However, there are some really good reasons why a new business should not borrow money – which I'll explain in this chapter.

BORROWING MONEY MAKES YOU LAZY

Don't you just love the Bank of Mum and Dad? There's not much, if any, paperwork and they lend on very favourable terms. Borrowing money from rich (or richer than you) benefactors makes you not think about ways to create and make money. But to quote Dale Beaumont of Business Blueprint fame:

'If you can't make money without money, you'll never make money with money.'

Dale's view is that borrowing money makes you lazy in business.

RAISING FINANCE TAKES TIME AND ENERGY

Following this theme, raising capital takes time and energy and that is time and energy you should or could be spending on the business. Raising capital is a distraction.

Often people start a business to gain a level of freedom – just think of all the so-called 'Mumpreneurs' or the semi-retired who want the flexibility to look after the grandchildren or play golf on Wednesdays, or the social media bloggers who like travelling.

If I were to provide capital to your business, how happy do you think I would be if you told me you were going on holiday for three months or that you had just bought a new car?

BORROWING MONEY OR RAISING CAPITAL REDUCES YOUR FREEDOM

You can say goodbye to autonomy! Some lenders will demand not only a return on the money, but also input into the decision-making. This is even the case for large businesses that list on the stock exchange – they then have shareholders to answer to.

To make decisions, people need information. So several times a year, at least, you are going to have to provide investors (or even the bank) with reports, plans and other information for them to make informed input into *your* business. Not only that, they will also expect their opinions to be implemented and, if not, you will need to explain why not. Being indebted slows down decision-making and for new businesses this is the time they need to be agile.

IT COULD COST YOU YOUR REPUTATION

'Your reputation is like a shadow, following you wherever you go,' said author and small business expert Frank Sonnenberg. Hopefully the thoughts and lessons in this book will help you succeed in your new business, but the reality in Australia is that only 60% to 70% of micro businesses survive four years (yes, the figure for failure is a lot higher than you may think). If your business is one of the businesses that fails and you can't return the capital you've borrowed to get the business off the ground then you lose your reputation as well as your money. If the investors are your family or mates then you could also lose those relationships too.

YOU HAVE TO PAY IT BACK

The last reason for not borrowing money is that you have to pay back the loan. Think about that as part of the big picture. Think about all your outgoings. You have to pay for the cost of goods you sell, or pay people to deliver services, you have all the business overheads to pay for, you pay the GST you have collected from sales to the ATO, as well as tax on profits you make. Do you really also want to pay interest on a loan, loan repayments or dividends to external shareholders?

You only pay many of these outgoings if you make a profit, but that's why you're in business, right? Remember the discussion in Chapter 1?

Over time, if you have used other people's money to start up your business, the best decision may be to buy them out – this requires more money and you may not be able to afford to do this.

Now, this chapter has been a little negative but it is really important that you consider the realities and the longer-term ramifications of raising capital and borrowing money to fund a new business venture.

KEY POINT: There is a time and a place for capital investment but I think this is usually when the business is more mature and even then it has to be done with a strategic vision and planning in place.

CHAPTER 19

Smart ways to protect your cash flow

We've talked already about the importance of cash flow to the health of your business. I showed you in Part 3 of this book how to calculate ratios to check your financial performance. In this chapter, I explain ways you can protect your cash flow.

YOU HAVE TO ACCEPT CREDIT CARDS

Have you ever gone shopping with a list and just cash? I bet you came home with only the things on the list and probably some change in your hand too. Compare that to going shopping without a list or cash and just a credit card. What did you spend then? What does this anecdote tell you about the power of credit cards?

There's no doubt about it, you'll make more sales if your business accepts card payments. The use of cash and cheques is declining and card payment use is inversely increasing. If your business doesn't accept cards, including credit cards, you will start missing out on sales. People spend around 15% more when using credit cards. If you sell online, it is almost a prerequisite to accept credit cards.

Credit cards are convenient for your customers

Here's an example of why you need to accept credit cards.

I had a guy, 'Mo', who came to look at the motorised gate at my home. I sent the enquiry online from my desk at my city office. Mo rang me from outside the house and gave me a quote then and there and I gave him the go-ahead to fix the gate.

Before I arrived home that night, I had received an electronic invoice and I was able to pay him by credit card that night. If Mo had only accepted cash, either I would have had to get someone else to come and look at the gate, or Mo would have had to come back to get paid. I would have had to get cash out of the bank and be home when he came back to pick up his money.

People want convenience and seek out businesses that accept credit cards.

Some credit cards offer users airline frequent traveller points or discounts and rewards and customers will seek that out as well.

Accepting credit cards adds legitimacy to your business

Have you ever had someone come and do a job for you and has asked to be paid in cash, and as they leave you think to yourself that they will just pocket the cash and not declare it as income? Or they might not actually be who they portray themselves to be – they look a little shady?

If a business or tradesman accepts card payments, especially credit card payments, it adds a further degree of legitimacy to their business.

Receiving card payments means you get paid faster

Credit cards benefit the functioning of your business. Cheques can take a few days to clear, cheques and cash require a trip to the bank which takes both time and people out of the business (and time is a lost productivity cost and lost opportunity cost). Credit card providers offer cash-back protections whereas cheques can bounce. All in all, your cash flow is improved if you accept credit card payments.

Don't worry about the fees

I often hear business owners complain about paying the transaction fees on credit cards.

Let me give you a scenario.

I go to the local shop with $200 in my pocket – the most I can spend is $200. Say the shop's margin is 30%, they could make $60 from the sale.

Now, say I go to the shop with a credit card and spend $300. The shop still makes its 30% margin – $90 – and pays the credit card company a 2% transaction fee (2% of $300 is $6).

So, I have a choice. I can make $60 from a $200 cash sale or $84 from a $300 credit card sale – that's an additional $24 profit. Even better, I might be able to charge the credit card fee to the customer – e.g. as car parks and airlines usually do.

What would be worse, though, is if the customer walked down the road to a competitor that did offer credit card payment.

SEND A LETTER OF ENGAGEMENT

How many times have you felt a little anxious and apprehensive prior to sending a customer or client an invoice? You've been scared of their reaction, nervous that their value of your product or service may not align with the invoice that they receive. Like most problems in life, this is usually a communication problem.

If you are a service provider, like I am, then prior to commencing work with a client, it's a good idea to send an engagement letter and ask them to sign and return it. The engagement letter should outline the purpose, scope and output of the engagement, the fees and when invoices will be sent and be required to be paid. When a client has to overtly do something, they become very aware of their obligations and usually there is never any further discussion about invoices.

When I have contractors working for me on an engagement, I sometimes have them complete a 'session checklist'. The session checklist outlines the tasks they complete, any issues they come across, additional work or items that will require further attention or work. The session checklist is emailed both to the client and to me. I am then aware of the work completed and any issues and so is the client. I allow the client 48 hours to respond or else I send the invoice based on the session checklist.

It is a little easier when you sell a product as the customer knows what it will cost prior to purchasing the product.

DIRECT DEBITS

Some businesses, such as gyms or lawn-mowing businesses, which provide regular ongoing goods or services, can set up direct debit payment arrangements with their clients.

If your customers are paying via direct debit, you avoid the following tasks:

- You don't have to send out weekly or monthly invoices
- There's no need to send reminder notices
- No-one pays late.

Of course, that's in a perfect world. However, with technology and direct debit, you almost do have a perfect world. Your accounting system should be able to send automated invoices and receipts, and an automated text message can be sent to remind your clients that their payment will be coming out of their account on a certain date.

Most banks can provide you with the ability to direct debit customers and there are other providers such as PaySmart in Australia that can do this too.

Direct debits also have the advantages of freeing up administrative time, stabilising cash flow and making your customers more loyal and 'sticky'.

MAKE IT EASY TO GET PAID

You need to give your customers as many alternatives to pay you as possible.

I was out and about in my car and thought I'd better get a 'filler' for my wife's birthday present – a store voucher card. I had one small problem, though, as I was standing in the shop looking at the stand of gift cards, I realised I didn't have my wallet on me.

However, it wasn't a big deal because I have an iPhone and Apple Pay, so I go up to the counter to pay. But this store didn't have paywave so I couldn't purchase the gift card.

What did I do? I jumped in the car and drove up the road to the nearest supermarket and made the purchase there. The original retail outlet lost a sale because they didn't have the technology that I needed to pay with.

You need to give your customers as many alternatives to pay you as possible.

Previously, I have put forward the case for why you should accept all credit cards, but what about if you provide the service at the client's site, for example, if you are a washing machine repairman?

Well, there are two suggestions:

1. *A portable credit card reader.* These can be obtained via your bank or there are PayPal and SquareUp readers that can be bought, which accept credit and debit cards.

2. *A tablet or smartphone invoicing system.* These allow you to complete the work, input the time and materials into the tablet program, have the customer sign the invoice on the tablet and press send. The invoice is then generated and sent and, if you're really sophisticated, your inventory and procurement systems are also instantly updated.

CHARGING UPFRONT

At Byronvale Advisors, we charge clients upfront when we're working with businesses on recoveries, rebuilds and restructures. No work is commenced until at least a day of time is paid for upfront. Why? Well, typically, these clients are already behind with their creditors and may be verging on being insolvent.

Getting paid upfront means we won't be waiting past a due date wondering when or if we will get paid. We will not be providing working capital to our client that costs us use of those funds. But it also means that if the client declares bankruptcy or goes into administration, we will not be a creditor and have never been one.

Therefore, we will not be caught up in the determination of which creditors get paid how much and when. If you are concerned about your customer or client's ability to pay you then save yourself a headache and charge upfront.

KEY POINT: The best way to protect your cash flow is to make it clear what the customer receives in return for their money and make it easy for them to pay you.

CHAPTER 20

Making sure you get paid

Chasing people who owe you money is not a pleasant task. People gravitate towards the tasks they like doing and procrastinate on the tasks they don't like doing. But let me ask you this – if you arrived home one day and your house had been burgled and the thieves stole several thousands of dollars' worth of your possessions, how would you feel? Pretty upset I bet. And you would report the burglary to the police and look at changing your security arrangements.

So why don't you feel like that when your customers or clients don't pay you for the goods or services that you have provided them with? Are you scared that you will lose the customer or client? If so, are they a customer or client worth having if they either do not pay you or pay late? Effectively, they have taken those goods or services just as the house burglar did.

In Chapter 8, we discussed cash flow forecasting. Customers and clients who pay you late are 'borrowing' your money as you have to have other cash available to cover your own bills, and that cash could have been utilised for something else. Or you have to borrow the money yourself to pay your own bills, or delay paying someone else and then you are effectively borrowing the money from them.

Customers and clients aren't your family or best friends. Would you be happy to lend an acquaintance the money? I suspect not.

Accounting software programs have features within them that automatically send reminder notices to customers. I find that this is OK for a few late payers, but I find picking up the phone and having a conversation is more effective.

This conversation, if managed well, will show the customer or client that you value them enough to take the time to call them. That, in turn, may help them prioritise your payment and, if you're lucky, it may also generate more sales (which you only process after they pay you for the work already completed).

But, what happens if the reminder notices and the phone calls still aren't working, and you are taking a lot of time chasing your money? What other avenues do you have?

PERSONAL PROPERTY SECURITIES REGISTER

Well, before you choose to trade with anyone, you can check The Personal Property Securities Register (PPSR). The PPSR is essentially an online noticeboard that anyone can access that shows whether someone is claiming an interest against goods or assets except for land, buildings and fixtures.

It may seem either scary or not something to do with your business but it is in fact there to protect businesses that:

- Sell goods on retention of title terms; or
- Hire, rent or lease out goods; or
- Buy or sell valuable second-hand goods or assets.

Here's how it can protect you.

If you are buying goods

By searching the register, you can check the goods you intend to buy are not encumbered in any way and are not going to be repossessed.

Say, for example, you buy a van for your business and do not check the PPSR. The seller could have financed the van and after selling it to you, he may not have repaid the loan. The finance company could then come and repossess the van and not provide you with any compensation. You should have checked the PPSR.

If you are selling on retention of title or consignment, or hiring or leasing out goods

By registering your interest on the PPSR, you have greater protection should your customer not pay or go broke.

If your customer does go broke then you are first in line to receive either your goods or monies back, instead of being an unsecured creditor waiting at the back of the queue to get only some of your money back, after all secured creditors are paid.

Some sale contracts have 'Retention of Title' or 'Romalpa' clauses in them that indicate that the goods remain the seller's until such time as the goods are fully paid for. However, it is likely that those who have registered their interest on the PPSR will be ahead of you in the queue and, in fact, the receiver may decide to sell the goods. Registering on the PPSR will strengthen your contracts.

The types of things that you can register on the PPSR are:

• Motor vehicles, boats and aircraft

• Crops, cattle and other livestock

- Stock in trade, artwork and equipment
- Other goods, new and second-hand, whether owned by businesses or individuals
- Intangible property such as patents, commercial licences, debts and bank accounts
- Financial property such as shares, cash or cheques.

The PPSR is available 24/7 and it is really cheap to register an interest ($6.80 for up to seven years) and search ($3.40 for one search).

CIVIL AND ADMINISTRATIVE TRIBUNALS

Most states and territories in Australia have a civil and administrative tribunal that can hear disputes about goods or services that you have bought or sold. In Western Australia and Tasmania, these cases are heard by the magistrates court.

The types of disputes heard by a civil and administrative tribunal are disputes:

- that arise out of the purchase or supply of any goods or service
- by persons or businesses or companies against each other in any combination
- for any amount of money (in Victoria – though other civil and administrative tribunals have similar)
- that arise or are connected to that particular state or territory
- that are under Australian consumer law for:
  - misleading conduct
  - unconscionable conduct
  - consumer guarantees.

Civil and administrative tribunals are the 'budget' version of taking someone to court. Lawyers and professional advocates are generally not permitted in the hearings and the filing fees are quite cheap. The civil and administrative tribunal also offers various alternative dispute resolution and mediation services.

STATUTORY DEMAND

A statutory demand is a notice made by a creditor under *The Corporations Act 2001* on a debtor company (note the debtor must be a company and not a sole trader).

A statutory demand is a useful way to pressure a company to pay its debts. There is, however, a clear set of steps that must be followed:

- The debt must be for more than $2,000.

- The statutory demand must be on the prescribed form and accompanied by an affidavit verifying that the debt is due and payable.

- The court can set aside a demand if there is a genuine dispute or offsetting claim (and this is a low threshold). A caveat – only use the statutory demand if there is a genuine dispute or else you may face indemnity costs.

- The service place for the demand is the registered office of the company being served. They have 21 days to apply for the demand to be set aside.

Once a company receives a statutory demand several things may happen:

- The debtor company pays the demand in full.

- The debtor company contacts you, the creditor company, and they negotiate a settlement.

- The debtor company applies to the court to have the demand set aside.

- The debtor company does not respond and you, the creditor company, apply to have the debtor company wound up.

So my layman's tip is that often smaller companies are not very diligent at keeping their registered address up to date with ASIC, and I have seen this used against creditor companies really effectively.

I was working with a client that received a statutory demand that had been sent to their registered office. The client had 21 days to either apply for the demand to be set aside, pay the debt, negotiate a settlement, or face being wound up.

The problem was they had not updated their registered office with ASIC and the statutory demand got sent to an address where they no longer had access to the mail.

Fortuitously, I was alerted to the fact although it was after the 21-day period. My client had a genuine dispute but as the 21 days had past they were unable to apply to the court to set aside the demand. This left them two choices: pay the debt or be wound up. My client paid the debt but this could have been avoided and, in fact, my client should have received money if they had only updated their registered address with ASIC.

DEBT COLLECTORS

When a customer or client has not paid a debt, or has exceeded credit terms, or when the debt is older than 60 days overdue and you have contacted them a couple of times and had no response or payment, then it may be worthwhile contacting a debt collector.

Debt collectors recover payments on behalf of clients that are legally owing to a business client. Outsourcing to a debt collector allows you to receive the cash sooner, focus on your core business rather than spending time chasing debts and it reduces your operating costs.

Once the debt is passed to the debt collection agency, the agency will handle the entire process. They will locate debtors, make contact with the debtor via phone, email, mail or in person, negotiate and collect payment and enforce any arrangements and manage litigation.

Usually debt collection agencies are only paid a fee if they recover the debt from a debtor. The activities of a debt collector are governed by the Australian Consumer Law and *Fair Trading Act* and the Australian Competition and Consumer Commission (ACCC).

Debt collection agencies are prohibited from recovering their fees from the debtor unless there is an existing contract between your business and the debtor allowing for the fees to be incurred by the debtor.

You are able to sue the debtor for the debt collection fees. However, if you lose, not only will you incur the debt collection fees but you will also incur your, and potentially the debtor's, legal fees.

Now, a caveat – make sure your data and information is both accurate and up to date. I have had a client that sent over 150 outstanding debts to a debt collection agency only to find their own accounting and payments system was not accurate or up to date. This resulted in additional work (though some of the additional work should have been done anyway) and loss of reputation with the businesses that 'owed' them monies.

FACTORING

Factoring is a financial transaction and a type of debtor finance in which a business sells its accounts receivables (i.e. invoices) to a third party (called a factor) at a discount. The origins of factoring were part of doing business in England as early as the 1400s.

When you factor an invoice, the factoring provider gives you funding in two parts. The first part is the 'advance' and it covers 80 to 85% of the invoice value. This is deposited directly to your business' bank account. The remaining 15 to 20% is rebated, less the factoring fees, as soon as the invoice is paid in full to the factoring company.

The main reason to use factoring is to receive the cash on your receivables sooner than the customer usually pays, for example you receive the majority of it today as opposed to in 60 or 90 days' time.

There are other benefits too:

- Factors provide the back-office support and manage the collection from your customers for free.

- Factoring is based on your customers' credit and not your business' credit.

- Factoring is not a loan so you do not incur a debt. Compare factoring with borrowing the cash from a bank via a loan and you would still need to collect the receivables and repay the loan – and incur a debt along the way.

- Factoring is scalable – the amount of funding can grow as your receivables (and sales) grow.

There are three types of factoring:

- recourse factoring
- non-recourse factoring
- reverse factoring or supply chain finance.

Recourse factoring essentially means you take responsibility for payment of the invoice to the factoring company, if they are unable to collect from the customer.

Non-recourse factoring means you 'sell' the invoices to the factoring company and the factoring company assumes all risks attached to the collection of the receivable from the customer.

Although recourse and non-recourse factoring are the most common types, there is also a type of factoring known as reverse factoring or supply chain finance. Here, the buyer sells their debt to the factor. The supplier benefits by being paid earlier and the buyer benefits by being able to manage cash flow and only has to pay one entity – the factor – rather than a number of suppliers.

Beware, there are costs in factoring. Firstly, factors only pay a percentage of the total invoice. Also, they usually have fee structures to have the factoring arrangement in place and these are typically for a 12-month minimum term.

STATEMENT OF CLAIM

A statement of claim is the start of a court action and is the action of last resort. I'd recommend you try the other methods that we've already discussed – one or some of them – before lodging a statement of claim. But for completeness, I will cover this subject off in this chapter.

Note that you should always seek your own legal advice on the information below.

A statement of claim is a form lodged at the magistrates court that outlines a factual description of why you believe money is owed to you. There is a prescribed format and you must include the date when the debt occurred, the place where the debt arose, a full detailed description of the events that demonstrate why the money is owed, recorded in numbered paragraphs.

The statement of claim is then lodged at the court either nearest to where the claim arose or the defendant's address. There is a filing fee and a service fee that must be paid at the court.

You will be issued with a case number and a date of filing. A copy of the complaint and two blank copies of notices of defence must be served on the defendant within 12 months of the complaint being filed in court. Anyone can serve the complaint, however there are some specific requirements that apply for service depending on whether the defendant is an individual or a company so you might consider using a process server. Once served, the defendant has around 28 days (this period may vary between jurisdictions) to lodge a notice of defence with the court and send a copy to you. No action can be taken during these 28 days. Once the complaint has been served, you need to provide the court with an affidavit of service, which details how and when the document was served.

A common question is what happens if the defendant is threatening violence when you try to serve the statement of claim. You don't need to put yourself at personal risk, so you can leave the statement of claim as close as possible to the defendant without putting yourself at risk. On the affidavit of service, you should describe the threats and where you left the statement of claim.

So, what happens next? That depends on what the defendant does. They may:

- File a defence
- File an acknowledgment of liquidated claim
- Do nothing – file nothing and pay nothing
- Pay the total amount on the statement of claim – yippee!
- Pay an amount that is less than the total on the statement of claim
- File a cross-claim.

If the defendant files a defence form, it basically means they dispute your claim and the case is headed to court as a defended case. There is a pre-trial review where both parties have an opportunity to settle.

If the defendant files an acknowledgment of liquidated claim, it means you are awarded the amount of the claim, plus costs and interest. The defendant can, however, make an application to pay by instalments so it could take months or years to get back the money you are owed.

If the defendant does nothing, you can apply for a default judgment. Default judgments need to be applied for within nine months of the defendant being served the statement of claim. If the defendant part-pays the amount owing, you can apply for a default judgment for the unpaid amount.

If the defendant pays the total amount on the statement of claim, either they need to file a notice of payment to the court, or you will need to file a notice of discontinuance.

Note: The statement of claim process is similar, but not the same, in each state in Australia. Information in this section is general in nature and has no regard to your personal circumstances. Information should not be relied on and the author is not liable for any consequence due to relying on information in this section. Please seek your own legal advice.

A BANKRUPT DEBTOR

If you are unfortunate enough to have a debtor file for bankruptcy or put their company into administration, receivership or liquidation, what are your options? They are different depending on the particular scenario.

* *If the debtor is bankrupt.* You cannot start a legal case for a debt after they become bankrupt. You might be able to get some money from the bankrupt's estate but if there are no

funds, the debtor's debt will be cleared and you cannot recover your money.

- *If the company is in receivership.* You can still make a claim in the court.

- *If the company is in administration or liquidation.* You can't start or continue a court claim unless you get permission from the supreme court. You can, however, lodge a proof of debt with the administrator or liquidator.

After you get a judgment in your favour, you still need to be paid. You have up to 12 years from the date of judgment to enforce payment.

There are a couple of enforcement methods (apart from instalment payments) you may consider. You could get a warrant to seize property or a warrant to deliver property. The warrant (and the Sheriff) will generally give the debtor an opportunity to pay the debt and, if the debt remains unpaid, it authorises the Sheriff's office to seize and sell items belonging to the debtor to pay the amount owing, as well as the creditor's court costs and the Sheriff's costs. You might also get an attachment order on the debtor's earnings. An example is getting the debtor's employer to pay you part of the debtor's wages or salary in instalments.

KEY POINT: Chasing people who owe you money is not a pleasant task but it is your money, so you can't afford not to. There are avenues to pursue though if debtors do not pay.

CHAPTER 21

How to have a holiday and still be making money

If I had a dollar for every time I heard people say they are either too busy to have a holiday, or they couldn't leave it to others to run the business while they were away, or it wouldn't be a holiday as they would be tethered to their emails and phone calls and disengaged from their families, I'd be able to go on holiday and still make money.

It doesn't need to be like that. Let me tell you a secret – the first of two secrets (well, 'secret' is probably the wrong word as what I'm going to tell you is what most small business gurus will tell you) – systemise your business!

Michael E. Gerber of the *E-Myth* books fame, Dale Beaumont from Business Blueprint and serial business author of the Business Secrets Exposed books, and Koos Kruger author and founder of the *Business Exit Companion* all give this advice.

Let's take a look at an example.

Larry the Landscaper is super busy and works around 100 hours each week. He gets up, goes to work, comes home and either falls asleep in front of the TV or drags himself straight to bed.

As we have discussed, Larry is working *in* the business rather than *on* the business and he has really created himself a job and not a business.

Larry's philosophy at coping with the workload, or not coping as is probably the case, is 'just do it', rather than figuring out how to get the work done through using other people who use innovative systems to produce consistent results.

Now, I concede, in theory this is easy and in practice it is hard, but it takes continual steps forward to climb a mountain. So, make time to systemise your business.

SYSTEMISE YOUR BUSINESS

Josh Kaufman in his book *The Personal MBA – Master the Art of Business* describes systems as:

> '… a process made explicit and repeatable – a series of steps that has been formalised in some way. Systems can be written or diagrammed, but they are always externalised in some way. The primary benefit of creating a system is that you can examine the process and make improvements. By making each step in the process explicit, you can understand how the core processes work, how they are structured, how they affect other processes and systems, and how you can improve the system over time.'

Systemising is the process of documenting everything you do in your business – from answering the phone and opening the mail, to pricing work and after-care service. There are many ways to do this and some aren't as daunting as you might expect. Here are some ideas:

- Over the course of a week write down what you are doing – sort of like keeping a log book. Use short sections of time and be quite specific. Use this as a starting point to document the tasks you do every day.

- Use voice, video or screen capture technology to document the tasks, e.g. answering the telephone.

- When training someone, get them to document the task they are undertaking and then review and refine it. This might take several iterations.

- Create an intranet site where your documentation and videos can be stored and accessed from anywhere. It's very easy to do this. You create a Google Sites account and then a sub-domain to your website with the URL going to Google Sites.

- Make a start. The most energy you spend to get something moving is getting it to start.

So, what does documenting and systemising your business do for you? Here are some of the advantages:

- It clarifies your thoughts and relieves stress.

- It can be used to train staff and provide a resource for staff to refer to, which will increase your staff's confidence.

- It makes you question if there is a better way to do something (part of working on the business rather than in the business).

- It creates the ability for a task to be replicated the way that you want it to be done, without you actually doing it.

- It lets you guarantee the quality of work because your staff will follow the same process.

- Your uniform processes are simple to audit.

- Staff will feel relieved because there is structure.

- It lets you sit on a beach in Bali knowing that tasks are being performed the way you want them to be done.

Without putting systems and processes in place, your business will become all-absorbing, with endless tasks to complete – like painting the Sydney Harbour Bridge.

However, when faced with the reality of their all-absorbing tasks, or finding an alternative, most business owners would rather live with the frustrations and endless tasks rather than risk enduring new, short-term frustrations of systemising their business.

Systems and processes allow others to share the load. These people then become what a studio recording is to Taylor Swift. A Taylor Swift song can be played by millions of people all at the same time. It sounds the same every time it is played and Taylor Swift collects a royalty every time the recording is played. Create a recording – a system – of your business, your talents, your way of doing something and then, like a song, replicate it, market it, distribute it and manage the revenue.

Without putting systems and processes in place, your business will become all-absorbing.

CREATE AN ASSET

Here's the second secret – if you systemise your business, you are creating an asset and increasing the value of your business. The value of that asset, your business, is directly proportional to how well the business operates. How well your business operates is directly proportional to the effectiveness of the systems you have in place and upon which your business depends. Your business no longer depends on you, your staff or other people, but on the systems.

As I have alluded to throughout this book, most small businesses are actually not a business but a job for the owner. What would happen if something happened to that owner and they couldn't work for a period of time? Say they had an accident and couldn't work? Sure, they might have income protection insurance that would pay them during the period they were out of action, but what happens when they are ready to start work again? There are no jobs in the pipeline and customers and clients have moved away from your business and found alternative service providers.

What happens if you decide you want to sell up and retire? A lot of small business owners have not even thought that they could sell their business, and when they retire they are happy to just know that their customers or clients will be looked after. It hasn't occurred to them that their business could be worth a lot of money.

You probably have an idea about what your business is worth to you but that is based on your earnings (I think of it as a salary for the owner for doing a job – not for building a business). Without you, though, there are no earnings so any prospective purchaser is only going to pay for the value of the assets such as any tools and machinery they are acquiring (and probably at a fire-sale value). Systemising your business creates an asset – a business – that can be replicated without you. And then you'll start to see the value of your business increase. Let me illustrate.

Henry is a sole trader home handyman. He has an operating profit of $100,000, which has been steady for the last five years. He also owns tools and a van worth $20,000.

Henry pays himself the whole $100,000 as a dividend each year. Henry wants to sell the business and retire. What is the business currently worth?

Without systems in place, the maximum value of Henry's business would be $20,000 – the value of the tools and van. With systems in place, the value of the business could be several times the operating profit plus the tools and van.

So, if Henry spent one day a week for a year systemising his business then his operating profit may drop that year, say to $70,000. But his business might be worth $300,000. For a $30,000 investment, he is getting a return of $300,000 – sounds like a good investment to me.

As a handyman, Henry could begin to systemise his business by following the steps listed earlier in this chapter.

There are many different ways to value a business but the bottom line is a business is only worth what someone else is prepared to pay for it.

Systemising your business creates an asset – a business that can be replicated without you.

PART 6

Essential business resources

CHAPTER 22

Starting a business checklist

I've deliberately made this section quite brief. However, there is a lot of information to get your head around. There are very good free resources provided by government agencies to assist businesses to get up and going, and a number of advisers in each of the areas below.

I've also deliberately left this checklist until the end of the book. Having read the majority of the book by now, you may well be thinking that starting a small business is not for you. You may feel overwhelmed, or your gut is telling you not to go ahead with starting a business. That's OK – in fact, it's good. It's better that you've made a well-informed decision and you can still review that decision in the future.

WILL IT BE A HOBBY OR A BUSINESS?

All businesses start as a small business and a lot of small businesses start off as hobbies. So, what is the difference? A hobby's primary purpose is to provide enjoyment and fun. A business is primarily commercial in nature and the purpose is to make a profit. Another distinction is that a business is an activity that is planned, organised and carried out in a business-like manner.

Once you have decided whether the activity you are undertaking will be a business, you should assess whether it will be viable or feasible. The Victorian government has a free booklet called *Planning and Starting Your Business – A short guide for new starters* available from www.business.vic.gov.au. It includes a ten-question quiz to help you self-assess if your business idea is feasible. If a business is feasible, it is realistic and workable – not only from a financial perspective.

HAVE YOU CONSIDERED THE POSITIVES AND THE NEGATIVES?

Let's be real, starting and running a business is not all milk and honey. There are negatives attached to the venture and there are positives too.

Positives of starting a business include:

- You make your own decisions – you have some freedom.
- You choose where you work and who you work with – both suppliers and customers.
- You get to run the business the way you want to.
- You hire and train the people you want and not those who are already there.
- You don't make a payment of goodwill for an existing business.

The negatives are:

- Getting the initial funds to commence and operate a business may be difficult.

- New businesses must create a demand for their product or service.

- It may take months or years for a new business to become profitable.

- Researching, planning and establishing a business can take a long time and a lot of money.

- You are an unknown quantity – suppliers may not extend credit to you at first.

The key point is that starting a business compared with buying a business entails a lot more work, cost and research.

HAVE YOU THOUGHT ABOUT THE STRUCTURE?

There are three typical business structures used by new businesses:

- sole trader;

- partnership; or

- proprietary company.

Which structure you use will depend on several factors: What type of business will it be? How many people will be involved? How will the profits be shared? What will be your legal liability? How will the tax be paid? Where do you envisage the business in the future?

Sole trader

If you are in business by yourself and envisage the business to stay that way, then you will probably elect a sole trader structure for your business. If the business grows, you will generally need to move to a different structure.

As a sole trader:

- you benefit from all profits and capital (goodwill) growth;

- you have low start-up costs;

- there is no legal separation between the business and the owner, so potentially your liability is unlimited and extends to your personal assets; and

- profit (and losses) from the business are treated as part of the owner's personal income. There are not separate tax returns for the owner and the business.

Partnership

You choose the partnership structure when two or more people start a business. In lots of ways, it is like a sole trader structure in that a partnership is not a separate legal entity. The partners' liability is unlimited and can extend to personal assets. The partnership does not pay tax, rather the partners pay tax on their share of the partnership income.

The partnership does need its own tax file number and must complete an annual tax return showing the allocation of income to each partner.

I recommend a partnership agreement be drawn up upon establishment of a partnership to avoid any disputes in the future, if this is the structure that you choose.

Proprietary company

A proprietary limited company has shareholders who own the business and directors who run the company on their behalf. You only need one shareholder and one director and it can be the same person – it can also be you, the person who starts the business. A proprietary company is a scalable business structure and has the following features:

- Shareholders' liability is limited to the amount invested in the company.

- It is a separate legal entity that pays tax on its profits at the company tax rate. The company has its own ABN and tax file number. Owners are either taxed on their income as employees or they pay tax on directors' fees or as dividends distributed.

- Compliance costs are higher, e.g. you will need to pay an annual ASIC company statement fee and pay for an accountant to prepare the company's annual tax return.

Note that with a proprietary company, consultants and contractors are still subject to the ATO personal services rules. However, with a diversified client and revenue base this structure may allow business owners to build up capital in the business and also potentially lower their average tax rate (tax advice should be sought from a tax agent though).

WHAT ABOUT A NAME FOR YOUR BUSINESS?

The structure you decide upon for your business will dictate how you register its name.

If you wish to operate as a sole trader you can simply use your own name, e.g. Stephen Barnes Consulting, and you don't need to register it. Any other business name (for example, Byronvale Advisors and Books by Byronvale) has to be registered.

When you register a business and company name, you have to check that the name is available to be used, unique and preferably easy to remember. Think about how it will stand out and emphasise what you do, for example Essendon Lawn Stencilling and Dyeing. Check the proposed name at the ASIC National Names Index and Australian Trade Mark Online Search System, and maybe also check the domain name availability.

Registering a business name is quite cheap and can be done at the ASIC website. 'Business name' and 'trading name' are also the same thing. You might, for example, be Stephen Barnes trading as (T/A) Essendon Lawn Stencilling and Dyeing on invoices.

Registering a company name is a similar process to registering a business name, however the company name must also indicate the legal status of the company, e.g. proprietary or Pty for companies not listed on the stock exchange, and the liability of company members (shareholders) e.g. Limited or Ltd. Byronvale Advisors is a proprietary company with limited liability for the shareholders hence the company name is Byronvale Advisors Pty Ltd.

HAVE YOU CONSIDERED TAX IMPLICATIONS?

Successive governments promise 'no new taxes' and attempts are made from time to time to 'simplify' Australia's tax system. But the reality is that taxation in this country is complicated, most businesses seek professional help to make sure they are compliant, but still, business owners need to be across it broadly. The tax-related matters you will need to consider are listed below.

Tax file number (TFN)

All businesses in Australia are required to have a TFN to complete an annual tax return. Sole traders use the same TFN as their personal TFN and partnerships, trusts and companies are required to have their own, separate TFN. You can apply for a TFN at the same time as you apply for an ABN.

Australian business number (ABN)

Every business in Australia needs an ABN. It is used to register for GST, PAYG, FBT and a range of other taxes (see below).

Also, when you deal with other businesses, your ABN must be quoted (e.g. on invoices). If you do not quote your ABN on invoices, businesses that make payments to you must withhold 46.5% of those payments and include them on their BAS return.

Goods and services tax (GST)

GST is a consumer tax whereby the last consumer in the supply chain pays the tax. You are required to register for GST if either your current or projected annual turnover is $75,000 or more, or you operate a taxi or hire car regardless of the turnover. You can, however, elect to register for GST even if your turnover is less than $75,000 (and $150,000 for not-for-profit organisations). Registering for GST also requires you to complete a business activity statement (BAS) either quarterly or monthly. You can apply for GST registration at the same time as applying for a TFN and ABN.

Pay as you go (PAYG) withholding

Any business that has employees must register for PAYG with-holding as this is the tax you withhold from earnings that you pay your staff.

Fringe benefits tax (FBT)

FBT applies to employers who provide benefits such as allow-ing a work car to be used for private purposes or paying for certain types of entertainment expenses to employees, including working directors or associates (e.g. family members).

Wine equalisation tax (WET)

WET applies to manufacturers, wholesalers and importers of wine (whichever is the last wholesale sale of the wine before GST is added).

Luxury car tax (LCT)

LCT applies to retailers, wholesalers and manufacturers of

luxury cars (with a sale value of approximately $57,000) at the point at which the car is sold.

Excise duty

Excise duty applies to businesses that deal in alcohol, petrol and tobacco products made or produced in Australia.

Stamp duty

This applies to those businesses dealing with land, motor vehicles or hire purchase transactions.

Land tax

Owners of land with a taxable value of $250,000 or more are required to pay land tax.

Payroll tax

Employers who pay wages over approximately $45,800 per month or $550,000 per year are required to pay state payroll tax.

HOW WILL YOU PROTECT YOUR INTELLECTUAL PROPERTY (IP)?

First of all, what is IP? Well, according to the IP industry body, IP Australia:

> 'IP is the property of the mind or proprietary knowledge. It is a productive new idea you create. This can be an invention, trademark, design, brand or even the application of your idea.'

Your IP may be something as innocuous as your business name. I registered 'Byronvale Advisors' as a trade mark. Why? Because there was a consultant in Australia with the name Byron Vale and I did not want him to trade as Byron Vale consultant or advisor.

Registering a business name, a company or a domain name does not automatically give you the same rights as registering IP, and you may not even have the right to use that name as a trade mark. If Byron Vale had registered 'Byron Vale' as a trade mark, Byronvale Advisors Pty Ltd could have been prevented from trading as Byronvale Advisors, even though the company name is registered. Likewise, if I had not registered 'Byronvale Advisors', anyone could have registered the domain names www.byronvaleadvisors.com or www.byronvaleadvisors.com.au and there is nothing that I could have done about it.

As your business gets bigger, the importance of your IP also grows. All those intangible things that can differentiate you from your competitors increase.

It is very important to keep your ideas, trade marks, design and patents confidential until you have your IP registered. Until it is registered, ensure anyone you talk to about it signs a confidentiality agreement. Don't allow any tweeting, posting on Facebook, blogging, publishing in magazines, or discussing at conferences. Zip it!

Registered IP is an asset that can be commercialised by assigning your IP to someone else (and getting a lump sum payment for it), licensing your IP (giving someone else permission to use it), franchising, or via a spin-off company.

The process, the cost, the length of registration process, the time the registration is valid and where the protection applies, varies depending on the type of IP and where you wish it to apply.

WILL YOU NEED COUNCIL AND PLANNING PERMITS OR LICENCES?

Every local council in Australia has a range of bylaws, zones and permit requirements and unfortunately these are not standardised.

Where you operate your business, the type of business and the size of business will determine the applicable council permits required. Examples of permits include:

- Building permit;

- Planning permit (for zones);

- Registration of food premises;

- Permit for tables and chairs on footpaths;

- Advertising signs; and

- Sale and serving of alcohol.

If you play recorded music and/or live music is performed at your business, then you are legally required to obtain an APRA AMCOS licence. There are a variety of licences that are tailored to different types of businesses and the use and frequency of the music being played or performed. Did you know that even playing background music in the non-public areas of your office requires a licence? Information on licences can be found at http://apraamcos.com.au/music-customers/licence-types/.

Another consideration is for home-based businesses that may require a council permit. Generally, a home-based business will not require a planning permit if:

- The home is your main place of residence.

- The total floor area used for the business is not more than 50 square metres, or one-third of the total floor area of the home.

- The business employs no more than one person who does not live there.

- The business does not use more of the property's utilities – such as electricity, gas and water – than normal domestic usage.

- The business does not decrease the attractiveness or value of the neighbourhood, e.g. it doesn't make excessive noise.

- Only one commercial vehicle less than two tonnes is registered to a resident on the property at any time.

- Nothing is offered for sale from the premises except goods made or repaired onsite.

- Goods are not displayed so they are not visible from outside the property.

- No vehicle is serviced, repaired or fuelled on the property.

Indigenous businesses can register as an Indigenous Corporation under the *Corporations Aboriginal and Torres Strait Islander Act 2006* (CASTI Act).

Under the CATSI Act, your business will operate under rules that take into account Aboriginal or Torres Strait Islander customs and traditions. You'll also be given the ability to operate nationally (as opposed to being limited to the state or territory in which your business is registered).

REGISTRATION INFORMATION MADE EASY

OK, so there is a long list of red tape and it seems a job in itself understanding and keeping up to date with all the requirements. But the Australian government has an online service designed to help you set up, expand and manage your business. To do this go to https://account.business.gov.au/, create an Australian business account (ABA) and register free to this online service.

Your ABA connects you to your local, state and federal government business obligations. It's delivered by a partnership of all three levels of government. You can use your ABA to:

- receive updates about changes to regulations;

- find and save the regulations that relate to your business;

- reduce your paperwork by pre-filling forms;

- apply for a range of licences online;

- keep a record of the forms you've submitted online;

- receive updates about new tools, events and webinars;

- be kept in the loop about ways to increase your bottom line; and

- get updates about opportunities in your industry.

WHAT INSURANCE WILL YOU NEED TO TAKE OUT?

Let's face it – insurance is expensive, especially when you're first setting up a business. Insurance, though, is important. What would happen if you were sick, lost your stock or premises in a fire or you were burgled? What would happen if someone was injured by a visitor to your premises, or your clients sustained financial loss caused by your supply of services or advice?

I advise clients to use an insurance broker for all their insurance requirements. Brokers know what insurances you need, the level of cover necessary and they obtain quotes from a range of underwriters for you. They usually offer reduced exclusions compared to what would be offered to you if you went direct to the underwriter.

Some examples of insurances your business may need are:

- *Building and contents.* This protects your business premises against damage and loss.

- *Public liability.* This insures for personal injury sustained by customers, clients or visitors to your work premises.

- *Professional indemnity.* This insures for your clients' financial loss caused by your supply of services or advice.

- *Business interruption.* This provides cover in the event your business cannot operate due to an event such as an earthquake. It is sometimes called business income insurance. The income loss covered may be due to disaster-related closing of the business facility or due to the rebuilding process after a disaster and provides money to pay for overheads, leases and staff costs.

- *Product liability.* This insurance covers you for injury or damage caused by products you sell, manufacture or supply as a service.

- *Cyber insurance.* This covers a business to recover after a cyber-related security breach or similar event. This is particularly relevant to businesses that collect or hold customers', members' or clients' personal information.

- *Intellectual property insurance.* This cover defends your intellectual property against infringers or defends infringement claims against you.

Note also that for home-based businesses, the standard home and contents insurance policies often do not adequately cover them. The public liability part becomes void when a business is started on the premises.

If you employ workers in your business and/or make yourself an employee, then you are required to have WorkCover Insurance. A business that pays, or expects to pay, more than $7,500 in wages, salaries, superannuation and other benefits, or employs apprentices or trainees, is required to have Workcover Insurance.

WorkCover Insurance may also apply to contractors and directors who may be classified as employees for WorkCover Insurance, where it is deemed the contractual arrangement is akin to an employment relationship.

There are essentially three tests:

1. The provision of materials or equipment is not the principal object of the arrangement.
2. At least 80% of the work is performed by the same person.
3. At least 80% of the contractor's overall services income is earned from the hirer.

ARE YOU PREPARED FOR THE END OF FINANCIAL YEAR (EOFY)?

If it's your first year in business, you may not be aware of a number of small things businesses can do to not only make the financial year end go smoothly, but also position the business for success for the next financial year.

EOFY checklist

This is a checklist of some of those items – each small – but collectively they will make a big difference.

Have you reconciled your accounts?

Make sure all your accounts are up to date up until the end of May, so that it is not a big job at the end of June. The reconciliation process will help ensure items are accounted for correctly and doing the reconciliations early gives you more time to sort out any unreconciled items, rather than rushing in the first few days of July. Accounts receivable and payable, bank accounts and payroll accounts are some normal accounts that can absorb a lot of time to reconcile.

There is also a right way and a wrong way to do reconciliations. If you are unsure how to do a balance sheet reconciliation correctly, ask your accountant or auditor. Asking the auditor is a way of learning the correct way and it will save your fees when you undergo the audit. If you don't have an auditor who can help then you can contact Books by Byronvale http://books bybyronvale.com.au/resources/ for a short video about how to correctly do a balance sheet reconciliation.

Is your invoicing up to date?

Ensure all invoices are entered in the accounting system and not sitting in an in-tray, a drawer or an unopened envelope. Also, ensure that all sales invoices have been sent. If you are getting behind, either block some time out in your diary or get a temp in to help you. You will have more time to get up to date before 30 June than after.

Accrual, depreciation and provision entries can be posted prior to month end, making just one less thing to do at the end of financial year.

Also get ready for a stocktake. A stocktake will allow you to write-off any obsolete stock and investigate any theft or shrinkage. Also, take advantage of any write-offs, deductions and rebates. Review your asset register and be aware of the small business instant write-off and deductions which currently applies on all purchases up to $20,000.

You might consider doing a 'soft close' at the end of May (or the penultimate month of the financial year). A soft close is effectively doing everything for financial year end up to May – that way you have done most of the reconciliations, sorted out and corrected the majority of problems and it will make the June 30 close a lot easier and faster.

Start preparing and writing reports and commentaries for financial reports prior to the end of the financial year. You will have most of the information you need and, where you don't, you can easily go back and insert the information.

Are you ready for the tax office?

Sole traders should make sure they know what deductions they can and cannot claim on their tax returns. Prior to each financial year end, the ATO usually 'advertises' areas they are focusing on through their website, in the newspapers and in their newsletters to tax agents. With regard to your expenses, the tax office will want to know that:

- You have spent the money yourself;
- The expense is related to your job;
- You have a record to prove it.

Each year, more than 650 million pieces of data are reported to the ATO by third parties including banks, employers, health insurers, state and federal agencies and overseas treaty partners. They know more than you think. Each year, the ATO contacts about 350,000 taxpayers about errors or omissions in their returns. The ATO raised $950 million in liabilities from reviews/audits of these types of deductions in the 2015-16 financial year.

Have you backed up your data?

Make sure you have a back-up and secure data outside your accounting system. Also, once your accounts have been finalised, save all accounts relating to the financial year so that the data remains accurate (and then also back up that data outside the accounting system).

The financial year end is not all about the financial numbers. It is also an opportunity to assess all parts of your business against your business strategy and plans. Being organised and planning ahead will ensure that not only will the financial year end process go more smoothly and without as much stress, but also you will set your business up better for the upcoming financial year.

CHAPTER 23

Glossary and list of abbreviations

ABA – Australian business account.

ABN – Australian business number issued by the ATO.

Accounts payable – the amounts owed to suppliers by the business.

ACCC – Australian Competition and Consumer Commission.

Accounts receivable – the amounts owed to the business by its customers.

APRA AMCOS – Australian Performing Rights Association Australian Mechanical Copyright Owners Society

ASIC – Australian Securities and Investments Commission.

ASX – Australian Securities Exchange.

ATO – Australian Taxation Office.

CEO – chief executive officer.

Content assets – forms of marketing content that can be utilised in inbound marketing, e.g. blogs, videos, eBooks, podcasts.

Cost of goods sold – the cost to get your product or service to the customer before taking into account your operational costs.

Creditors – a person or company to whom the business owes money.

Current assets – cash and other assets that are expected to be converted to cash within a year.

Current liabilities – bills that are owed by the business to creditors and suppliers within a short period of time.

Debtors – a person or company that owes money to the business.

FBT – fringe benefits tax.

Goodwill – the amount of value attributable to the business above the fair value of the net assets.

Gross profit – revenue less cost of goods sold.

Gross profit margin – gross profit divided by revenue.

GST – goods and services tax.

KPI – key performance indicator.

LCT – luxury car tax.

Net profit – profit after taking into account all costs.

Net profit margin – net profit divided by revenue.

Operating expenses – costs such as administrative expenses and costs that cannot be attributed to a single product, e.g. electricity, rent, stationery. Also exclude depreciation and interest costs.

Overheads – all operating costs other than cost of goods sold. Also includes costs that cannot be attributed to a single product unit.

PAYG withholding – pay as you go withholding – a tax system that involves regular payments made by employers and other payers such as superannuation funds. It is used to collect by instalments income tax, and a range of other government charges such as student loan repayments and Medicare.

Personal property – most sorts of property that is not land, buildings and fixtures.

Personal Property Securities Register (PPSR) – a national 'noticeboard' that shows whether someone is claiming an interest against goods or assets.

Security – an interest in personal property which secures payment of debt or performance of another obligation.

SEO – search engine optimisation.

SME – small to medium enterprise.

Sunk costs – costs that already occurred in the past that can no longer be controlled or managed, e.g. patents, cost of incorporation, research and development.

SWOT analysis – analysis of strengths, weaknesses, opportunities, threats.

TFN – tax file number.

WET – wine equalisation tax.

Working capital – current assets less current liabilities.

Work in progress – the labour and material costs in a service-based business.

CHAPTER 24

Useful websites

In this chapter I'm including some useful websites. I'm not endorsing any of them, nor do I receive commissions or kickbacks from any of them. This is not an exhaustive list, so if there is something you want to know about, or you have any useful websites you think I might be interested in, contact me at Byronvale Advisors or post on our Twitter (@byronvaleadvise) or Facebook pages. You can also find this list on the Byronvale Advisors website www.byronvaleadvisors.com and we'll update the list on the website too.

The Byronvale Advisors website also scrolls the logos of some of our trusted partners. Click on the logos to go directly to their websites.

GOVERNMENT AGENCIES AND NGOs

.au Domain Administration – www.auDA.org.au – a place to find about .au domain name registrations, availability, and the difference between the secondary-level domains.

APRA-AMCROS – apraamcos.com.au – licences organisations to play, perform, copy, record or make available their members' music, and then distribute the royalties to their members.

Australian Business Account – https://account.business.gov.au/ – where you register for the Australian Business Account (ABA), to better manage all your government-related licences, permits and registrations.

Australian Business Licence and Information Service – www.ablis.business.gov.au – ABLIS helps you find the government licences, permits, approvals, registrations, codes of practice, standards and guidelines you need to know about to meet your compliance responsibilities.

Australian Business Register – www.abr.gov.au – The ABR stores details about businesses and organisations when they register for an ABN.

Australian Industry Productivity Centres – www.aigroup.com.au/member-services/productivity-centre – Australian Industry Productivity Centres (AIPC) provide services to help Australian businesses strengthen their operations, enhance their international competitiveness and tap into global supply chains.

Australian Securities and Investment Commission – www.asic.gov.au. ASIC has information on business names, and company and organisation details, registrations and governance and compliance requirements and forms.

Australian Taxation Office – www.ato.gov.au – The ATO has a pile of information, tutorials and videos on how to meet your taxation obligations.

Business.gov.au – www.business.gov.au – an online government resource for the Australian business community.

business.gov.au offers you simple and convenient access to all
the government information, assistance, forms and services
you need. It's a whole-of-government service providing
essential information on planning, starting and growing your
business.

Country of Origin Label – www.originlabeltool.business.gov.au
– free tool to produce the most applicable label for your
product.

INNOVIC (the Victorian Innovation Centre) – www.innovic.
com.au is a not-for-profit organisation assisting over 1,000
innovators and entrepreneurs each year. They offer a wide
range of practical services, free seminars and innovation
resources to help your business idea, innovation or enterprise
through all the stages of commercialisation.

IP Australia – www.ipaustralia.gov.au – Administers Australia's
intellectual property (IP) rights system, specifically patents,
trade marks, designs and plant breeders' rights.

Small Business Mentoring Service – www.sbms.org.au is a not-for-
profit that provides access to experienced mentors who have
the skills and experience to help small business. SMEs have
access to a free Business Review service to assess their
performance and identify opportunities for improvement.
Through this review, AIPC business advisers will be able to
help businesses upgrade their capabilities or find solutions to
technical or process issues.

The Australian Competition and Consumer Commission –
www.accc.gov.au – an independent Commonwealth statutory
authority whose role is to enforce a range of legislation
promoting competition, fair trading and regulating national
infrastructure for the benefit of all Australians.

The Department of Foreign Affairs and Trade – www.dfat.gov.au – provides support for Australian business, working closely with portfolio partners such as Austrade, Tourism Australia, ACIAR, EFIC and other agencies.

SOCIAL MEDIA AND INBOUND MARKETING

These links are specifically for using with Twitter, Facebook, LinkedIn and your own website to make your social media marketing easier.

BlogLovin – www.bloglovin.com – a tool for keeping up with blogs – a way to manage feeds. You can follow any blogger on any platform, whether or not they're also signed up.

ChatHeroes – www.chatheroes.com – Chat Heroes allows you to offer online customer service on your website through a manned live chat service that delivers profitable leads 12 hours a day, 7 days a week.

FatJoe – www.fatjoe.co.uk – outsourced link-building and content marketing agencies.

HashTagify – www.hashtagify.me – a hashtag search engine with data about hashtags.

Hootsuite – www.hootsuite.com – social media management tool that allows users to schedule and post updates to any pages or profiles for Facebook, Twitter, LinkedIn, Google+, Instagram, WordPress and others from one place.

Infogram – www.infogr.am – an easy to use infographic and chart maker.

InviteBox – www.invitebox.com – a referral program you can add to your website.

LeadPages – www.leadpages.net – landing page builder with accompanying suite of lead generation and opt-in tools.

Likealyzer – www.likealyzer.com – helps you to measure and analyse the potential and success rate of your Facebook Pages.

MailChimp – www.mailchimp.com – An email marketing service. If you have 2,000 or fewer subscribers, you can send up to 12,000 emails per month absolutely free.

ManageFlitter –www.manageflitter.com – a web-based application that assists Twitter users to gain insight into their Twitter account.

Referral Candy – www.referralcandy.com – refer-a-friend program that provides users several advocate invitation options such as email, post-purchase pop-ups, the ability to include links in a newsletter, or via manual and bulk invite options.

TweetDeck – www.tweetdeck.com – is a dashboard application for Twitter to manage.

Twilert – www.twilert.com – a Twitter search tool that sends you email alerts of tweets containing your brand, product, service and keywords.

Unbounce – www.unbounce.com – custom-built landing pages for your website.

Visually – www.visual.ly – handpick the best freelancers out there to help you produce high-impact infographics, videos, presentations, reports, eBooks and interactive web microsites.

Zapier – www.zapier.com – Zapier moves information between your web apps automatically.

ADVICE AND OUTSOURCING

Avast – www.avast.com – a family of internet security applications. The Avast Antivirus products include free and proprietary cross-platform versions that provide computer security, browser security, anti-virus software, firewall, anti-phishing, anti-spyware and anti-spam among other services.

Books by Byronvale – www.booksbybyronvale.com.au. An outsourced bookkeeping provider supported by the experience and team at Byronvale Advisors.

Byronvale Advisors – www.byronvaleadvisors.com. Your hands-on partner to accelerate your business to the business you have always dreamed it to be.

Canva – www.canva.com – a free graphic-design tool website, founded in 2012, by Australian Melanie Perkins. It has an easy to use drag-and-drop interface and provides access to over a million photographs, graphics, and fonts. It is used by non-designers as well as professionals. The tools can be used for both web and print media design and graphics.

Fiverr – www.fiverr.com – a global online marketplace offering tasks and services, beginning at a cost of $5 per job performed, from which it gets its name. The site is primarily used by freelancers who use Fiverr to offer services to customers worldwide.

HubSpot – www.hubspot.com – an inbound marketing and sales platform that helps companies attract visitors, convert leads and close customer. There are many such platforms but HubSpot offers a range of free products and training.

OnStrategy – www.onstrategyhq.com – strategic planning consultants and strategic planning execution platform.

PeoplePerHour – www.peopleperhour.com – an online platform giving businesses access to thousands of skilled freelance experts in hundreds of different fields.

Zoho Projects – https://www.zoho.com/projects/ – Plan, track, and collaborate using a project management portal. Good if using remote and outsourced teams.

Afterword

Throughout this book, I have tried to challenge the reader (in a nice way) on different aspects of their business – why they are in business, the impact of their decisions and the mental shift required from buying a job to building a business. And, as the title suggests, my objective is to teach you how to run your business better.

My aim (stated on the front cover) is to cover essential information every business owner should know and use: from planning, understanding key reports and ratios, pricing, marketing and getting paid. I haven't gone into great depth on any subject within the book as the point is not for it to be a 'how to' manual.

I recognise that every business, and every business owner, is different and unique, just as a teacher or a coach understands that each student or player is different and unique. However, I'd make a bet that there's one thing that almost all successful business owners have in common and that is a desire to run their businesses better. They are always looking at ways to improve.

I hope this book encourages you to look at your business differently and find ways to transform, grow and develop your business, to take both you and your business to the place you have dreamed of it going.

Now that you've read the book, get your significant other to read it too. Remember, every business is a family business. Then, and I can't emphasise this enough, actually make a start on running your business better.

I wish you every success with your business. If the book has helped you then please send me an email at feedback@ byronvaleadvisors.com and we can celebrate your achievement.

If you have any questions about some of the topics in the book in relation to your business please also do not hesitate to contact me.

Further reading

Australian Taxation Office – website and information for taxpayers and tax agents.

Good to Great by Jim Collins.

HubSpot Inbound Certification course.

IP Australia website www.ipaustralia.gov.au.

Planning and Starting Your Business – A short guide for new starters – business.vic.gov.au.

Purple Cow: Transform your Business by being Remarkable by Seth Godin.

Business Exit Companion: An Owner's Guide to Exit Planning and Unlocking Value by Koos Kruger.

The Complete Guide to Strategic Planning – OnStrategy – www.onstraqtegyhq.com.

The E-Myth Bookkeeper: Why Most Bookkeeping Practices Don't Work and What to Do About It by Michael E. Gerber, Debbie Roberts, Peter Cook.

The E-Myth Revisited: Why Most Small Businesses Don't Work and What to Do About It by Michael E. Gerber.

The Personal MBA: Master the Art of Business by Josh Kaufman.

The Seven Day Weekend by Ricardo Semler.

Acknowledgments

Thank you to all the incredibly talented colleagues and clients I have worked with over the years who have taught me so much, broadened my thinking and supported and trusted me.

To the incredible SMEs that have helped consolidate and affirm my thinking and from which I have drawn a lot of information in this book. You are my mentors and inspiration.

To my family, who often struggle with the ebbs and flows of the consultant's life and who have supported and trusted me through this journey – thank you with love.

To Lesley and the team at Major Street Publishing, thank you for helping me turn my vision and a rough manuscript into this book.

This book is dedicated to my daughters, Laura and Amy.

About the author

Stephen Barnes is the Managing Director of a boutique management consulting firm – Byronvale Advisors. A self-described polymath, he advises and consults to CEOs, boards, owners and their leadership teams in organisations from multinational corporates to start-ups and not-for-profits. He helps and shows his clients how to manage their businesses with a passion and specialises in helping businesses and organisations recover, rebuild and restructure.

Stephen's background is eclectic, which enables him to see the bigger picture and find solutions to complex problems.

Stephen started consulting to start-up businesses in 1991 as a 20 year old. He also built, owned and operated a café at this time to gain a better understanding of the issues facing start-up businesses. Stephen moved into the corporate world working in a range of industries and roles which were largely focused on processes, systems and problem-solving. He then moved back to his passion of helping organisations and businesses as a consultant.

He has been a director of many for-profit and not-for-profit organisations.

Outside of work, Stephen juggles the demands of his young family and enjoys 'Zen time' fly fishing when time permits.

Stephen lives in Melbourne, Australia and can be reached at www.byronvaleadvisors.com.